THE LAWYER WHO COULDN'T SIT STILL

To Diana

THE LAWYER WHO COULDN'T SIT STILL

Best wishes & thank you for inviting me.

Michael Simmons

Book Guild Publishing

Sussex, England

First published in Great Britain in 2011 by
The Book Guild Ltd
Pavilion View
19 New Road
Brighton, BN1 1UF

Typesetting in Garamond by
Norman Tilley Graphics Ltd, Northampton

Printed in Great Britain by
CPI Antony Rowe

A catalogue record for this book is available from
The British Library.

ISBN 978 1 84624 630 2

CONTENTS

AUTHOR'S NOTE

As a recently retired lawyer, I am all too aware of the risks of defaming my subjects, not to mention my heinous breaches of client confidentiality. For this reason, among others, I have endeavoured only to libel the dead, as they have no legal comeback. Where their living families might be hurt, or offended, I have used fictitious names, as I have also done to protect the not so innocent living.

I have tried to preserve as much client confidentiality as possible for the living, who are only identifiable by reference to matters already in the public domain, even if long forgotten, and solely available by painstaking research of dusty court records. I do thank the many who gave their consent, sometimes reluctant, to publication.

For the rest, I only hope they will forgive me for my present indiscretions, and remember our past friendships. My compulsive need to tell a good story outweighs, at least in my opinion, the lesser need for silence and tact. Most of it happened a long time ago.

Writing is a lonely business, but I must acknowledge the help that I have received. First of all my wife, Samantha, encouraged me throughout, and saw that I rose above my normal slapdash, journalistic standards. This book would not have appeared at all had my secretary of nearly fifty years, Joyce Reeves-Russell, not had the ability to read my tortured handwriting, a knack that I have not mastered myself. My old firm, Finers Stephens Innocent LLP, was particularly accommodating. The Practice Director, Philip Mitchell, mostly turned a blind eye to my use of office facilities for personal purposes, and Nitesh Bhagwan and his heroic staff in the post room cheerfully turned out at short notice beautifully bound copies of draft after draft of the book, as it evolved. Ronald and Gertrud Irving were constructively critical, and pointed me in the direction of my wonderful publishers, Book Guild Publishing, whose energy and efficiency inspired me, especially with their ability to answer my questions, even before I knew that I wanted to ask them! Needless to say, all the mistakes and infelicities are mine.

Michael Simmons

INTRODUCTION

I did not become a lawyer out of any sense of calling or commitment, but more by a process of elimination combined with the influence of an ambitious mother. Medicine was out, as I had no scientific background or bent. There were already far too many doctors in the family. At any wedding, if the cry went up, 'Is there a doctor in the house?' half those present seemed to erupt into movement, whether towards the casualty or the exit was difficult to calculate.

I abandoned the thought of accountancy, when I heard my mother's friend, May, proudly announce that her son, Anthony, with the accent on the 'th', was going to be an enchanted accountant. I resolved to seek my magic elsewhere.

Cambridge was either the making of me, or the destruction of me. Opinions differed. I found no great stimulus in academic law, and I was paralysed by incipient grief at the thought of leaving the place that had become a substitute womb. As a result, I made no effort to look for a job, when the inevitable time came to leave. In an ideal world, my parents would have been rich enough to support me in a postgraduate life, as idle as that which I had enjoyed as an undergraduate, but it was not an ideal world. The fact that I could have stirred myself academically to stay on to do research was something that never crossed my mind. I was unaware that, with a half decent, rather than a spectacular, Cambridge law degree, I could probably have had articles in one of the more prestigious law firms in London. In fact, I was so lacking in interest in the whole business that I did not even know that there *were* prestigious law firms.

I therefore left it to my father to explore his meagre contacts to find a solicitor who might be prepared to give me articles of clerkship. The signs were not auspicious. I reluctantly attended various interviews after trudging up endless stairs in insalubrious office buildings. The worst was the little hunchback, dressed in black coat and striped trousers, in his dingy office with a full set of golf clubs gathering dust in the corner, who was more concerned with what business he could get out of my 'daddy', than what he could do for me.

The best of a bad bunch was Beresford Alton, 'Bob' to his friends and 'the Major' to his staff, who was prepared to extract a hundred guineas from me in exchange for my slave labour for three years, coupled with the possibility that he would impart sufficient practical knowledge to help me pass my final exams. Bob was an interesting character. Born Boris Altschuler, he had been managing clerk before the war to Stuart Oldershaw, himself married to the daughter of Kenneth Levy. Bob had a good war, as the saying goes, and ended up with the rank of major. On his return, he was able to qualify as a solicitor with little difficulty, and was offered a partnership by Stuart Oldershaw, if he changed his name to something more acceptable. Never one to resist a challenge, Beresford Alton was the outcome.

The offices were on the top floors of a building called Rolls Chambers, off Chancery Lane. You noticed a slight and increasing lavatorial smell as you trudged up the linoleum-covered stairs. The theme continued in the rear, where there was an extraordinary, green, cast-iron urinal, which would have fitted nicely into the Science Museum. The staff consisted largely of old ladies, whose time was long past. There was an assistant solicitor, Scholes, who had been a prisoner of the Japanese, and was considered unreliable after lunch. He was not too good before lunch either, if I think about it.

There was also the particular bane of my existence, my fellow articled clerk, Monty Wernick. Monty was a 'five-year man' as he had not been to university. He had a distinctly Dickensian odour. He viewed it as his job to make my life as unpleasant as possible. Sadly for him, I had other ideas. I was smarting at the loss of my Cambridge existence, and having to live once more with my parents in Wembley, because I had no money, meant that I had a streak of suppressed savagery only waiting to come out. Monty, unfortunately for him, felt the full force of it. He swiftly learned to leave me alone.

The work was depressingly menial, but easy. In the morning, I filled in county court summonses, until it was time to go on my rounds. These included Bush House for stamping documents, Somerset House for probate and divorce work, and the High Court for writs, judgments and assorted issues. The clerks in the Queen's Bench Division were selected for their supreme sadism. A pettifogging exactness was required for filling in the forms. If you used letters rather than numbers or vice versa for what was required, your effort was rejected. Your document was always thrown back at you as soon as an error was detected, so you could go back and forth five or six times before the job was done. It was an exercise in constant humiliation, based on the fact that the clerks would be doing that job for the rest of their working lives, while at some stage in the relatively near future we articled clerks, like butterflies emerging from our chrysalis, would suddenly become fully-fledged solicitors of a far superior station and income.

Like medieval apprentices, the articled clerks spent much time together. In summer, we favoured the Oasis swimming pool near Holborn. One lunch time, I was enjoying a swim, when I suddenly remembered that there was £400 in banknotes for stamping documents in my jacket pocket, in those days a fortune, which I had left unguarded in the cloakroom. I shot out of the water like a dolphin to rescue my charge.

After a year of this life, I had left home, taken on various evening jobs to make ends meet, but was still virtually delinquent. I was

saved by the sudden disappearance of Scholes, the assistant solicitor. What happened to him was never explained. I was called in by
Bob Alton and asked if I would like to take on his workload. Needless to say, I was still expected to do the outdoor clerking, but I
would be paid overtime for the extra hours that I needed to put in.
I was assigned Miss Frost. She must have had a first name, but I
never found out what it was. She had been Scholes' secretary, and
before that had worked for Stuart Oldershaw. She knew all about
the form, but nothing about the substance of the law.

I sat down behind a Victorian desk, piled high with dusty, cardboard bundles, tied with pink tape. Everything was neglected and
in a complete mess. I set to work methodically to sort things out
with Miss Frost's help. My legal knowledge was scanty, but most
problems seemed solvable by the application of a little common
sense. I gradually established a working routine, and the very
shabby leather covering of my desk at last became visible.

Those two years passed very quickly. I hardly had time to realise
what valuable practical experience I was gaining. It reached the
point that Bob would go off on holiday and leave me to do his
work as well. I had the telephone number of a friendly solicitor
down the road in case I needed help, but I never called him. Do not
think that I did not make mistakes, I did. I hastened the bankruptcy
of one client by giving too much information in my innocence,
when his bank telephoned. I comforted myself with the thought
that he was going broke anyway. Believing that the Treasury
Solicitor's department was staffed only by honourable lawyers, I
agreed to terms of reference in an arbitration of the 'have you
stopped beating your wife' variety. Whatever the outcome, my client
could not win.

It was now time for me to leave the office and attend full time at
Gibson & Weldon, a crammer only graduates were allowed to use.
I suddenly realised that I liked the idea of a career in the law. I had
become that thing that as a student I never thought I would, an
ambitious person.

Such academic success as I had achieved up to that point had been gained by the expenditure of as little effort as possible. This was all now going to change. For the next six months, I devoted myself to studying as hard as I could for the first, last and only time in my life. If there were two textbooks on a subject, I read them both. I revised and then revised again. When I got an eye infection as a result of too much reading, I sat in the waiting room at Moorfields Hospital until my name was called, reading the small print of *Gibson's Conveyancing*.

It was all worthwhile, as I was placed equal first in the half yearly intake of potential solicitors from the whole of England and Wales and won a prestigious prize. I was now ready to practise law, but not any old law. I wanted to use my professional skills to travel. My problems were diagnosed early at school. 'Easily bored' was a recurrent phrase in my reports. I knew that everyday legal work would soon pall without something special added, and that I needed the 'spice' that regular travel would bring. I also found the international aspects of law the most interesting, especially those involving Conflict of Laws. Of course, the overseas trips were merely snatched interludes in the general scheme of things. A great deal of hard work was done onshore, to justify the occasional flight of fantasy offshore. I was always looking for the chance to travel, and my readiness to pack my bags at short notice was quickly appreciated by those clients who needed my services in that respect. I was lucky that so many of my trips were interesting adventures, and I did not find myself inspecting stranded freighters on remote sandbanks in God-forsaken places like Chittagong or Cox's Bazaar, the fate of a number of my professional brethren, who specialised in Admiralty work.

Two inevitable years spent as a very junior officer on National Service in the Royal Air Force gave me ample opportunity to perfect my plans. I was able to use my new-found academic distinction to land the job of my dreams, and a combination of luck, recognition of such talents as I possessed, and the desire of my then boss, Anthony Sumption, to pursue other business interests, left me at the age of twenty-nine as sole proprietor of a small city law firm with every opportunity to indulge my fantasies of international legal work and extensive overseas travel, subject only to the overriding need to earn sufficient to keep body and soul together.

1

FRANCE

Mood Swings and Extreme Generosity

Partnership with Anthony Sumption was an educational experience. He was subject to violent mood swings and rages. The staff were terrified of him. I had only been there a few weeks when I took a call from his wife. He was out at the time. When I next saw him, I told him that his wife had telephoned. 'That bitch,' he shouted. I was very much taken aback. By contrast, he could be absolutely charming. Six days of the week, he was a pleasure to know, but the seventh came without any warning with a black mood, when you tried to stay as far away from him as possible.

He was a brilliant lawyer, but a lousy solicitor. He did not like people, and he could not be bothered to make the effort to pretend that he did. He was fortunate in that he had been able to make a large sum of money in tax avoidance schemes, picturesquely named Dividend Stripping and Bond Washing. He had started out advising his clients on these schemes, and had then cut himself in as a principal to strip and wash with the best. He felt that his activities were sufficiently known to the Inland Revenue and disapproved of to ensure that his chances of future public office were zero.

As he became more confident in my ability to run the practice, he left me more and more to my own devices, which I enjoyed, as I found his mood swings difficult to bear. He was very much a sophisticate and bon viveur, and I realised that I still had a lot to learn about life. I was then, and remain to this day, grateful to him for giving me the chance to develop and spread my wings.

Anthony was increasingly taking time off and leaving me to run things. By then we were equal partners, but the disparity in our ages ensured that I did not feel any resentment that I was doing all the work, and he was receiving half the profits. I expect that, if this situation had continued for too long, I would not have been so happy.

He announced in June that he had rented a villa in the South of France, and planned to spend July, August and September there. I was not at all upset, as it gave me the chance to develop my skills and the practice even further. I had no holiday plans myself at the time. Off he went, and halfway through August I was surprised to receive a phone call from him, announcing that he was bored there, and planned to come back at the end of the month. He asked me if I would like to take the house for September. I knew that the rent must be a fortune, and I could not possibly afford it. I told him so, and he replied that I should not be silly: the rent and other expenses were all paid in advance, and it was a gift from him to me. I was overwhelmed by his generosity and of course agreed.

On my last Friday in the office before setting out for France, I was working late, trying to organise work for the others after my departure as efficiently as possible, when I received a call from one of Anthony's friends, who informed me that he had to return the four tickets for Glyndebourne for the next evening that Anthony had given him. I told him to send them round to the office, and resolved on the spur of the moment to use them myself, as there was no time to do anything else with them. We made up a strange party: Judy, my then wife, Jeffrey Stern, an eccentric academic from the London School of Economics, and his girlfriend, Jean. He kept telling us how they were going to play 'mining engineers' that night. After the opera, we drove to Brighton, and chose to spend an uncomfortable night on the pebble-covered beach under the stars, punctuated by a sole trumpeter playing 'Early Hours' again and again.

The next day, Judy and I set out in my ten-year-old Alvis. It had been a beautiful car but it was now nearing the end of its natural life. The doors were framed in wood, and you merely had to coax them shut. I used to wince inwardly whenever a passenger treated them like the doors of a modern car, and slammed them. When I was in the Air Force, stationed at Uxbridge as a very junior adjutant, I used to have the car lovingly racing tuned by the Motor Transport Section gratis on a daily basis. The year before, we had driven it across Europe as far as Yugoslavia, but the warning signs were there. On this trip, we had left Calais behind, and were driving in the rolling hills of Normandy when disaster struck. The car just stopped for no apparent reason. I tried every trick I knew to restart it but without success. I left Judy to guard the car, and set off along the road in the noonday heat to find help. There had been no human habitation for some time behind us, so I thought it best to be an optimist and go forward.

I found a village, where everything was closed, and managed to extract a dubious promise from the local garage, after disturbing the proprietor's lunch, to send out a mechanic, when he could be found. I trudged back very dispirited up and down the hilly road with the tar, and me too, melting in the heat of a lovely summer afternoon. As I breasted the final hill, I assumed I must be witnessing a mirage. There, to be sure, was the Alvis with its bonnet up. There also was Judy, but there too was a white repair van with a mechanic, impeccably dressed in white overalls, poking about in the entrails of my car. He turned out to be a racing driver named Richard Shepherd-Barron, who was on his way to Monza with his wife, Penny. He had seen Judy by the roadside, and stopped to offer his assistance, which was more than welcome. He restarted the car, and we invited them to come and stay with us on their return at Le Canadel.

I wish I could say that the rest of the journey passed without incident, but it was not the case. The bonnet blew off somewhere in the Massif Central, and we had to tie it back on with string. Furthermore, an electrical fault developed, which meant that the lights went out whenever I changed gear. This made night driving, especially on windy roads, a little hazardous!

Our arrival at Villa Silvaplana caused considerable consternation. The concierge and his wife came out to greet us. The look on their faces said a lot. The French are such natural snobs despite their Revolution. They were accustomed to Anthony's pristine and often chauffeur-driven Rolls-Royce. It was obvious what they made of our dusty, battered old Alvis with its bonnet held on with string, and its shabby and travel-stained occupants. The villa was amazing. There were five bedrooms and the same number of bathrooms. It was set in its own secluded orange grove leading down to a virtually private beach and the sea. There was a charming note of welcome from Anthony to say that everything was paid for except the telephone, but including the contents of the wine cellar, which he urged us to drink.

What was extraordinary during the next four weeks was the behaviour of most of the friends whom we had invited to join us. They seemed to be consumed by envy at our new-found status. We knew that it was only a temporary and exceedingly generous windfall, while they assumed that we were set at this standard for life. It was not a pleasant experience in that respect. The worst was a couple who made off with our supply of toilet rolls. The best was my friend, Edgar Biss, with his languid cello-playing girlfriend, Camilla, from Sri Lanka, who practised being languid, while he cooked us marvellous meals.

The drive back was uneventful, and we returned sunburnt, relaxed and extremely grateful to our benefactor, Anthony Sumption. As I arrived at the office on Monday morning there was Anthony with a face like thunder. 'What happened to my Glyndebourne tickets?' It took me some time to remember and understand what he was talking about. When I told him what I had done with them, he stated that he would instruct the office cashier to debit my account with the cost, a paltry £16. I replied that he need not bother, and wrote him out a cheque on the spot. My senior partner was a man of paradoxes.

2

IRELAND

Living the Life of Royalty

When Harold Allen came to see me, it was already too late to save him and his wife from bankruptcy. It was a sad story, and one that is still repeated so often. Harold and Isabel had both been junior career naval officers. Her speciality had been catering. They had fallen in love, married and quit the Navy. They opened a restaurant called the Swordfish at Gosport, and the combination of Harold's bearded, bluff, ex-naval charm front of house, and Isabel's inventiveness and efficiency in the kitchen created an instant success. The restaurant was soon in all the guides, and they were making substantial profits.

Sadly, Harold decided that he was the complete businessman, and invested the profits in a ten-pin bowling franchise in the nearby Lee Tower. His timing was bad and the franchise was making increasing losses to the point where the restaurant could no longer sustain them, and the creditors of both businesses were becoming increasingly insistent.

Having written off the Allens in every sense, I was surprised to receive a very strange telephone call from Harold some months later. 'Michael, I have to keep my voice down, as I am in a very public post office in Ireland and can be easily overheard. How good are you at negotiating with royalty?' I paused, as anyone would, before answering that particular question. 'As good as the next man, I suppose.' 'Fine,' he replied. 'I'll be over next week and tell you all about it.'

It transpired that the Allens had decamped to Ireland. In their travels up the west coast, they had reached Sligo, and then came upon Classiebawn Castle, which was owned by Earl Mountbatten. Harold was struck by its potential as a very up-market private hotel. At the time, it was used by the Earl's family for a short period for holidays in the summer, but otherwise it was on the books of an exclusive letting agency in New York. When it was let, Mountbatten's steward and other staff looked after the guests. Harold, who did not lack chutzpah, wrote to Mountbatten as one naval officer to another, a former lieutenant to a former admiral of the fleet, outlining his proposal and suggesting a meeting. He received a short, sharp, negative reply, but it was followed a few days later by a much more encouraging letter suggesting a meeting at Mountbatten's London home.

Once Harold had briefed me, the meeting was arranged, and he and I duly presented ourselves at Mountbatten's tiny mews flat in Kinnerton Street in Knightsbridge. The larger mansion behind had been sold off years before to support the family's extravagant lifestyle. Crammed into a tiny living room were Mountbatten himself, his son-in-law, Lord (John) Brabourne, other family members, his solicitor, his secretary, his assistant secretary, Harold and me. To say we were outnumbered was an understatement.

Mountbatten told us that his change of heart was caused by the sudden death of his steward. American guests were expected that summer and, if the Allens looked after them, they could take their own paying guests, when there were no Americans, as a trial run. If that was successful, he was prepared to enter into a three-year lease for the Allens to take on the castle as an exclusive private hotel from next year. Mountbatten's solicitor and I were left to draft the documents. Mountbatten expressed an interesting caveat. We had to go easy on the local staff from Easter, when the season started, for a month or two, so that they could regain their strength. They were not paid during the winter, and therefore starved! What he did not know, as I discovered later, was that the locals exacted a telling revenge. They used to hop over the wall round the estate, cut down and remove the trees, and then sell them back to the castle for firewood at an exorbitant price.

Listening to Mountbatten in best naval style asking those around him for their views ('What do you think, John? What do you think, Gerald?'), I realised how he had partitioned India. It was all a question of the quality of the staff work. The information would be provided to him and he would make the decisions. Nice, straight lines were always preferable. It had obviously been faulty information in India, as three million Hindus had been left on one wrong side of the border, and two million Muslims on the other, all of whom had lost their lives in the massacres that predictably followed

Knowing that Harold had no money, and I had no chance of being paid for my services, I resolved to be the first guest once Harold and Isabel had taken up their posts, and there were no paying Americans in sight. Sure enough, Harold telephoned to announce that there were three weeks vacant over Easter. I told him that we were coming. The party consisted of Judy, our two small boys, Daniel and Oliver, Eileen, their large nanny, and me. Squashed into my bouncy Citroën, we set off across eternally rainy Wales to Fishguard. The ferry to Cork was an adventure for the boys, but I did not relish standing on the quayside at Cork and watching my car being hauled out of the ship's hold by crane, perilously suspended in the air, and then dropped, none too gently, on the quay.

The drive up the west coast was beautiful, but I kept forgetting to go slowly. The effect of the peat bogs on either side of the road was to cause the tarmac to rise in unexpected bumps. Poor Eileen was sitting in the middle at the back between the boys, and every time we hit a sudden bump she was lifted up, and hit her head on the roof. As we reached Sligo, the countryside was becoming wilder. The sight of Ben Bulban, still with snow on it, reminded me that I should have shown more appreciation for Yeats at school.

Classiebawn looked as if it had come straight out of *Grimm's Fairy Tales*. Built in the neo-Gothic style in Victorian times, it had come into the Mountbatten family from Lady Edwina's side. I mused that this was another example of Jewish money – on this occasion from the Cassel family – refreshing the coffers of the British aristocracy. The Allens were pleased to see us, but the welcome from the Irish servants was more restrained, and this attitude persisted throughout our stay. The Irish may now be republican to the core, but the snobbery acquired from working for the English aristocracy also ran deep, and we were clearly not of the class to which they were accustomed. I recalled that Mountbatten in London had told us about the butler, Frank, who only got drunk when there was no queen in the house. I helped him to bed during our stay on numerous occasions.

Judy and I were allotted the Lady Edwina suite. Mountbatten had of course been a widower for many years. The books by the bedside were a strong reminder of where we were, and the previous occupants of the room. The best was *A Book of British Birds* compiled by HRH Prince Philip, which had written on its flyleaf 'To Uncle Dickie on his birthday from Philip'. I was tempted, if not to add it to my collection, at least to sell it to a second-hand bookshop, but I resisted. Everywhere were reminders of royalty. The place mats, on which the staff grudgingly served us our meals, were emblazoned with the family coat of arms. The long-playing records in the living room followed the theme. Elgar's 'Pomp and Circumstance' and the 'Coronation Suite' were clearly played more often then Sinatra or Cole Porter.

To get some peace away from the squabbling children, I went for a long walk one day on Mullaghmore beach. This is an extraordinary expanse of flat sand, which stretches for miles. I covered a large amount of ground at great speed with the wind behind me, and then I turned round to retrace my steps. The Atlantic gale nearly knocked me over. At that moment it started to rain as well, and it was a great pleasure when I at last got back, soaked to the skin, to dry out before a blazing fire.

We received few visitors, but news travels quickly in a remote place like this, and people were curious to see the strangers from

England. The local priest, Father Flynn, was an engaging character. On his arrival, while I went to the pantry to fetch him a drink, Judy entertained him in the living room. 'Do you ever go dancing?' was his chat-up line. It seemed that celibacy in the clergy was not a concept that had got as far as Sligo.

The subject of alcohol was a delicate one. We had no licence, and Mountbatten was concerned about this, to the point that we had a strict confidentiality clause concerning it in our agreement. The local police were equally interested. I took a phone call one day from Sergeant O'Hara of the Garda, who announced that they were about to raid us. This gave us time to put everything alcoholic out of sight, before two police cars with blue lights flashing and sirens blaring came storming up the drive. They were all extremely friendly and installed themselves in armchairs after a perfunctory search. 'Would you like a cup of tea?' I asked. 'We would prefer something stronger,' was the reply with a twinkle in the eye, so we brought up the contents of the bar from the cellar, and spent a merry evening privately entertaining our new friends.

I had to visit Sligo to see Mountbatten's local lawyer, Harry Brown, whose firm was called Argue & Phibbs, one of the best names for a law firm ever. Our next visit to the town was for a pageant to celebrate fifty years since the Easter Rising in 1916. Accustomed as I am to the English rather half-hearted and wishy-washy version of patriotism, I was amazed at the fervour of the Irish. 'And the dastardly British did this – and the dastardly British did that.' It went on and on, and it was having an effect on me, ever the contrarian. I fancied the idea of standing up and singing 'God Save the Queen'. Then I took another look at the audience and decided not to do so. I would probably have been torn limb from limb

On the way back, we were due to spend the night in Dublin, but I had reckoned without the Horse Show. There was not a room to be had, until surprisingly the very popular Russell Hotel offered us one. There had to be a catch in it, and there was. The room was directly above the bar, and the singing, more often melodious than not, went on throughout the night. As we could not sleep at all, we joined in on the basis that, if you can't beat 'em, join 'em. We all had a good time, as well as our money's worth, in Ireland.

The story did not, however, have a happy ending. I suddenly received a worried call from Harold. Had I seen the *Daily Express*? I said that I had not, but that I would immediately go out and buy it, then ring him back. We knew that the Beaverbrook Press were no friends of Mountbatten, and there it was as the lead story in William Hickey. 'Mountbatten turns boarding house-keeper'. It was a lurid and overblown account of Harold's deal to run the place as a private hotel.

The next call was from Gerald Churcher, Mountbatten's solicitor. Could we attend an urgent meeting at Kinnerton Street? Harold flew over, and we went round the next day to be greeted by almost the same cast of characters. I was impressed that the Earl remembered my name. Apart from his matinee idol good looks, he had immense charm. More in sorrow than in anger, our experiment in hotel-keeping had to terminate with immediate effect. I was able to negotiate terms of settlement that were reasonable in the circumstances. The Allens went off to New Zealand to seek their fortune. I never heard from them again.

3

ITALY

Pure Chance Leading to a Lifetime Obsession

One of my problems in making a success of a legal career was that I was attracted to the wrong people. Instead of cultivating captains of industry and the exceedingly rich, I preferred to spend time with interesting riff-raff. Robin Cook fell into that category. Expelled from Eton at sixteen, and from a very rich family, which had disowned him, he made a living on the fringes of London society, and wrote lurid novels about his experiences. *Private Parts and Public Places*, for example, was about his time spent working in a Soho porn shop. His love life was equally dramatic; he met a black nightclub hostess on a flying visit to New York, married her the next day, and left her the day after. He then married the daughter of the proprietor of a Bloomsbury delicatessen, had a son, and abandoned them both. When I first met him, he was living with Sandra, the daughter of an Irish gangster. Sandra's father spent much time in hospital, as he was married to Daphne, who was a compulsive stabber. They all lived in a flat above a car showroom in Warren Street, until Daphne inadvertently left the bath running and the ensuing flood ruined thousands of pounds worth of expensive motor vehicles sitting below.

Eventually, London became too hot for Robin. He had offended the Chelsea Mafia in some way, and they, together with his ex-wives, were hot on his trail. He bought an old Army lorry, and he and Sandra loaded it with all their worldly goods, and then set off across Europe. The lorry finally expired just outside Roccatederighi, a remote hill village in Southern Tuscany. Robin was extremely tall and thin with all the charm of a born aristocrat. He did not speak a word of Italian, and the villagers had no English, but this was no problem to Robin. He bought a piece of derelict farm land steeply sloping down to a river, and persuaded a local builder, on a promise of payment some time in the future, to join two rustic houses into one by creating an extremely imposing vaulted living room in between.

Robin and Sandra settled down to their version of village life. Robin learned to speak Italian with a strong Tuscan accent. This, combined with his Etonian drawl, created a very strange impression. He was a prodigious drinker and this, among other things, endeared him to the locals. He was the uncrowned king of the village, and could have led them to war. He wrote about his life there movingly in a novel entitled *A State of Denmark*.

He was telling me about all this on a trip back to England. We were dining in Chelsea, and it was my misfortune to be sitting next to Daphne, who was moving ever closer to me, so that I feared she would soon be sharing my trousers. Robin extended an invitation to Judy and me with our two small boys to come out and stay in the village that summer. We drove down in a much more reliable car this time; but we only had a sketchy idea of where the village was. The address was given as Grosseto, which I knew as a town. I did not know that it was also a province. It was pelting with rain and we were all very tired. Eventually, I saw a man sheltering by the roadside, and asked him in my faltering Italian if he knew Roccatederighi. It transpired that he was going there, knew Robin, whom he called 'Mister Cooki', and was prepared to take us.

Robin had arranged for us to have two bedrooms in an apartment in the village, and we proceeded to have a wonderful holiday. They could not have been better hosts. We spent much time on the beach at Alberese, a remote spot in a wild game park, where there was the perfect fish restaurant. We spent many sleepy afternoons half watching the children make sandcastles, while we recovered from the effects of too much cool, white wine. Things went so well

18

that Robin issued an invitation to return next year, but this time to stay with them at Fontemeleia, their farmhouse. Judy, whose opinions I did not necessarily value, got it right on this occasion, as she wanted to stay once again in the apartment.

We arrived in the village and unpacked. We then walked to the local trattoria for dinner, and we learned of the difficulties that faced the village. Robin and Sandra had quarrelled, and effectively done a midnight flit. Their lovely, black Labradors, Oliver and Edward, had to be put down, as there was nobody to look after them, and worse was the state of financial havoc which they had left in the village. For the past eighteen months, they had lived totally on credit and paid no one. It was very easy to do, as I discovered later. If you went into the baker for a loaf of bread, and found that you had forgotten your wallet, there was never a problem. 'Pay tomorrow' was the inevitable response, and for Robin tomorrow somehow never arrived.

Our dinner turned into an informal creditors' meeting. One by one, sad-faced men came into the restaurant and presented me with their bills. They knew I was Robin's lawyer, and they hoped I could do something about their terrible financial plight. The builder alone was owed the equivalent of £1,800, a small fortune to him. When we arrived back in London, I found Robin, and persuaded him without much difficulty to let me sell Fontemeleia, pay off the creditors, and divide any balance equally between Sandra and himself. We had an argument about the price; he insisted that he only wanted to sell for what he had paid for the property or, more accurately, what he owed on it, rather than what it was then worth, which I reckoned was a far greater sum.

I put an advertisement in the Personal Column of *The Times* with my telephone number. The first call was from an extremely military-sounding voice. 'That property you have for sale, I'll buy it.' 'You mean,' I replied, 'you want to look at it.' 'No,' was the answer, 'I'll buy it.' Captain Ian Reid had been a regular Army officer in the Black Watch before the war, and was accustomed to making speedy decisions. He had been captured and had escaped no less than seven times in Italy, been sheltered by and fought with the Partisans, and knew the area well. Predictably, Robin changed his mind halfway through the transaction, but I exerted the force of my personality and insisted that he complete the sale. Ian Reid was very grateful to me, and stated that as a reward he wished me to be the first person to stay there as his guest.

By then, my personal situation had changed drastically. The shaky marriage to Judy had finally broken down, and I was living in somewhat straitened circumstances with Maggie in Highbury, as virtually all my income went to maintain Judy and the boys in the former matrimonial home in Highgate. We set out with friends to have a wonderful holiday. Up to now, I have said little about the village, as we used it for little more than sleeping, spending as much time as possible on the beach, or touring and visiting the more famous towns. Roccatederighi was 'Frederick's rock'. He had been the younger son of a Sienese nobleman. Because of the law of primogeniture, he would inherit very little, so had been encouraged to go off with his small band of retainers, and seek somewhere else to colonise. He was looking for a high place, which could be readily fortified, where there was a spring to supply fresh water. This was his chosen spot. They captured some local women, and cattle, to found their community. I had hardly looked at the old village, which was perched on the rock itself. The church was at one end and the clock tower at the other, with crowded houses and narrow alleys in between, all higgledy piggledy without any obvious plan and everything built in the grey, local stone called trachite. From afar, it looked a little like the rock of Gibraltar. The lower village, where the trattoria, bars and shops were situated, had grown up much later, and that was where our flat was to be found.

Maggie was keen to see the old village, so we climbed up, one hot day. It was a fairly dismal sight, at least to me. The village for many centuries had served as a dormitory for miners. At its peak, there had been no less than fourteen bars serving a population of less than four thousand. They had mined both coal and iron, but sadly there had been several disasters with much loss of life, and the State had closed down the mines, and pensioned off the miners. Everybody who had somewhere better to go had left, and those who remained spent most of their time sitting in the square in the lower village gazing into space. The upper village had been largely abandoned to rot.

We found ourselves in a derelict square near the clock tower at the top of the village. There was rank grass growing everywhere from cracks in the concrete and fissures in the rocks. Opposite us were two abandoned cottages without windows. They reminded me of men without eyes. Clearly, the roofs were also in terrible condition. 'They're beautiful,' said Maggie, 'we must buy them.' I looked around to see if she was looking at some other property, but no, her attention was fixed on these two.

We asked around in the village, and eventually the local poet, Sileno, appeared with the keys. To me, the houses were as horrible inside as out, stinking of damp and decay, but Maggie, in her mind's eye, saw only the finished product. We bought the two houses for the princely sum of £400, which even I could raise, despite the problems of my divorce.

We decided to go back to Mario Magnanelli, who had been Robin's builder and whom I had saved from bankruptcy by my efforts. Maggie gave him a detailed specification of our requirements, and I gave him £600 on account. As we rounded the final slope the following year, I said to Maggie, 'There will either be a palace to see or nothing.' There was nothing. The only concession to building work was a small heap of sand outside the front door. We went to see Mario, and asked him why he had not carried out our instructions. His answer was illuminating: 'You went away: how did I know that you were ever coming back?' That was the state of mind of the typical villager, and there was no answer to it. We got our deposit back and moved on to the next builder, who was recommended by our lawyer in Grosseto, Giorgio Padovani. The problem with this builder was that he was not used to working in the hills as all his customers were in the city or on the coast. He did not understand the extreme weather conditions that the village experiences in winter, so his work was largely wasted.

It took a total of fifteen years and five builders in all before the property was completed to our satisfaction. By then we had added on other bits, and become as completely integrated in the village as any foreigner could be. I have helped organise international music festivals, quarrelled violently with the mayor, processed through the village streets dressed in medieval costume as the captain of our local *contrada* in the Roccatederighi version of the Palio of Siena with donkeys substituted for horses, and made many good and lasting friends there. Our children, too, view it as home, and perhaps their children will in time become true Rocchigiani.

4

BANGKOK

A Shock to the System

You would not easily trust John O'Brien. An Australian horse dealer, who was unable to return to Australia for unspecified reasons, he had a salesman's gift. His brother, Robert, remained in Australia, and bought the horses, which John sold. They seemed to have a telepathic understanding of a bargain in horseflesh. He came to me on recommendation, because he had made a contact in Thailand, and was interested in all sorts of international business beyond mere horse-trading. As the weeks passed, these interests expanded to take in property, finance, commodities, advertising and public relations. John was using me as one of his contacts to assemble a suitable team to make a visit to Thailand.

He assured me that he was dealing with a reputable Thai government organisation, and that it would pay for our trip and all our expenses. Frankly, I did not believe a word of it, but I went along with John's enthusiasm in case I was wrong. The air tickets arrived just three days before we were due to depart. This precipitated a frenzy of activity. On the more mundane side, I had to submit to all sorts of painful injections, while we had to organise meetings to introduce the team to each other and devise some sort of strategy.

We were a motley group. Carl Schwartz was a financier allegedly recommended by Barclays Bank. He claimed to be of German origin, but spoke English with a parody of a French accent. His accompanying accountant spent all his time checking up on the truth or otherwise of Carl's more extravagant boasts. He never caught him out, but he was getting near. There was also Carl's lawyer, who was a bit too stiff and inflexible for this sort of jaunt. I resented the presence of a second lawyer and determined to try to run rings round him. There were two advertising men, who also seemed a bit surplus to requirements, a typical public relations man, John, myself and Jenny, a New Zealand secretary, whose presence was unexplained. The obvious inference was that that she was sleeping with John, but that was not the case.

As we were dealing with a top Thai government agency, we were likely to be introduced to royalty. We needed to take a present to the King and Queen. Somebody came up with the brainwave of a pair of corgis, a breed so beloved of our own dear Queen. John went out and bought them. It was agreed that we were likely to be subjected to all sorts of temptations to soften us up, including carnal ones. We agreed that we would have to display a British stiff upper lip at all times.

I remember the trip to the British Overseas Airways terminal in Victoria far too well. I was carrying an extremely heavy suitcase with an arm throbbing with the result of the recent injections. The first stop was at Frankfurt, and I had the task of rescuing the corgis from their cage and walking them on the tarmac in temperatures well below zero in the teeth of a howling gale.

We next refuelled at Delhi at the height of tension between India and Pakistan. The airfield was surrounded by slit trenches and barbed wire. There were armed sepoys with fixed bayonets everywhere. When one of our party was unwise enough to bring out a camera to take a picture, he was pounced on, had his camera impounded, and was nearly incarcerated himself.

We arrived at Bangkok airport exhausted in steamy heat, to be greeted by a smiling delegation and marched off to a lounge where we were interviewed under hot lights for television. If we did not know it before, we now knew that we were celebrities. The drive to the hotel passed in a daze. The Petchburi Hotel did not seem a five-star luxury establishment, but my room was comfortable enough. I went out onto the balcony to see immense water buffalos wallowing in a swampy pool below.

We did not have much time to rest, as we were told by our welcoming hosts that we were due out for dinner very soon. I was just lying down for a moment, when there was a knock at the door. I opened it to find a smiling, young page-boy. 'Hello, sir, you like your suit pressed?' 'Yes,' I replied. 'You want your shirt laundered?' Once again, I replied affirmatively. 'You like a nice girl?' I was surprised, but explained that we were soon due to go out for dinner. 'Oh, short time then,' he quickly improvised. I got him out of the room, and realised that I could learn a lot here about point of sale techniques.

I dressed carefully for dinner, including powdering my socks and shoes liberally to combat the effects of the heat. We arrived at a very luxurious Chinese restaurant, and I was a little taken aback to see that the custom was to take off your shoes before ascending the thickly carpeted stairs to the next floor. There was nothing I could do but leave snow-white prints all the way up those stairs, yeti-like, to announce my arrival.

We now had the chance to meet those responsible for our trip. The General was a short, slim, military figure in impeccable dress uniform. His English was excellent, as he had spent a lot of time on training courses with the British Army, including time at Sandhurst. He was a minister in the government, and wished to follow in the footsteps of his fellow ministers by establishing personal trading links with business entities run by other governments, so as to enrich himself personally. I quickly realised that his was a case of mistaken identity, as our group could in no way fit that category.

His sidekick, Vinay, did not conform to the same stereotype. He was short, squat and with a villainous cast in one eye, which ensured that you could never be certain if he was talking to you when he looked at you. We were told that in future we would see little of the General because of his ministerial duties, but that our day-to-day contact would be with Vinay. Frankly, I held out little hope of a happy outcome. The meal was delicious, but I had a problem. We were supposed to eat with chopsticks. No other cutlery was available. I had never previously mastered that particular art, but the food was far too hot to pick up by hand, supposing that was permissible, and I was ravenously hungry. I there and then learned to eat with chopsticks.

The next day was scheduled for a business meeting. Everyone sat round a big table. I was dreading a very boring day, but I was reprieved, as I was asked to draft an overarching cooperation agreement between the two sides. They still thought we were a respectable governmental mission, while we were quickly learning that they were a bunch of opportunistic cowboys. I put something very flowery together starting with the words 'Whereas as accredited representatives of our two great nations, we wish to cooperate to mutual benefit in investment and trading operations'. Jenny typed it and we covered it with red sealing wax. It was then bound with lashings of green silk. It was not worth the paper it was typed on.

I listened in for a bit to the boring and purposeless discussions that were taking place round the table. It was a case of the semi-blind leading the blind. As I saw no place for me there, I claimed extreme jet lag and returned to my room for a short time, but soon made for the pool. There were a number of lean, tanned, crew-cut American Air Force officers already there, and they told me that Bangkok was the 'Rest and Relaxation' destination for those fighting in Vietnam. We saw it more in the early evenings as we sat drinking in the bar. One wing of the hotel was set aside as a short-time brothel. Taxis would draw up, and out would step tiny, Suzy Wong-type figures in their brilliant plumage, accompanied by tall and extremely young American males. The average encounter lasted twenty minutes. The American would stagger out looking dishevelled and blinking in the sunlight, to be followed a few minutes later by his former companion, who looked completely composed, and ready for her next customer. Many of the girls were back with another American boy – they were little more than that – about thirty minutes later, and the whole process would be repeated. You could not blame the men. They were more than likely to be blown to smithereens, when they returned to Vietnam, and they did not want to die virgins.

That evening, after another dinner with Vinay and his colleagues (they considered it as their duty to eat with us), we went to a night club, and what a night club. The bar area was swarming with Suzy Wongs. As soon as we sat down, we were surrounded. After our pep talk before the trip, I expected us to shoo them away like flies. I was wrong. We all had 'companions' sitting on our laps, and we were busy buying them and ourselves drinks. My own companion seemed to have a great sense of humour, as she laughed at everything I said. As I drank more of the so-called 'whisky' provided, she became more and more attractive. Despite our language difficulties, we became good friends..

I cried off the continual business meetings, and announced that I wanted to go shopping. Within an hour my telephone rang to announce that my car was outside waiting. It was an air-conditioned white Cadillac, driven by a uniformed soldier with his similarly dressed companion to act as my guide and carry my shopping. I was happy to let the rest of the group continue their discussions, which I was convinced would lead nowhere. I shopped until my soldiers dropped. I had brought a dinner jacket with me, and I resolved to have it copied in raw Thai silk, as I had heard that their tailors were excellent. I must have been unlucky, as my new dinner jacket ended below my knees. I looked like a Teddy Boy in it.

That evening, after another solemn dinner, we went back to the same night club. I saw Thip, my companion from our previous visit, chatting up an American soldier, but she soon joined me. She invited me next day to her house for tea, and I was eager to see how the other half lived. There was no doubt that our group was living in the lap of luxury, and I suspected that there was another side to life here. I went in a three-wheel tuk-tuk. Provided that you remembered to hold on tight, it was an excellent form of transport, even if exhaust fumes were not as pleasant as my air-conditioned Cadillac of the morning. Thip had a small wooden house near the

Floating Market. It was spotlessly clean, and I was greeted by her servant, who removed my shoes. I had learned my lesson, and my feet this time were not over-powdered. We sat quietly drinking tea, and I could not help contrasting this time with our time spent in the club and after. We were joined by her youngest sister, whose fees she was paying to go to a good school in Bangkok. Her sister was beautifully dressed in a school uniform consisting of a white blouse and a pleated, navy-blue skirt. She bowed before me as an important visitor to her home. It transpired that Thip was one of a family of fifteen children in Chiangmai. There was little work, therefore Thip had been sent to Bangkok with her pretty, older sister to earn money as night club girls to support the family. There was none of the usual Anglo-Saxon prudery or evasion of the nature of the work involved. The directness of Buddhism was a refreshing change from the morals which I was used to at home. As soon as she could, Thip had sent for her youngest sister and, as she earned more, others would follow to be educated.

It was clear that there was a downside to the life the girls led. Thip told me that her elder sister had become pregnant, and that the American serviceman involved had been promptly shipped out. She was going to collect her sister and the baby from the hospital tomorrow, and she asked me, as her friend, to come too. We went by a proper taxi, and I was first shocked by the grounds of the hospital. They were covered with fires, where family groups were cooking meals for the patients, as the hospital did not provide any. The ward, where Thip's sister was, was no better. There were beds everywhere: closely-spaced beds on either side of the room, and beds in the middle. Beds lined both sides of the corridor. I had not seen such a press of humanity outside a football stadium. We took Thip's sister and her new-born baby to her home. This was an even bigger shock. We had to gingerly cross a plank over an open sewer, which stank, to get there. There was a kind of barracks, and the sister's quarters consisted of a tiny curtained-off cubicle. I noticed in passing that the barracks backed on to the canal, where tourist boats approached the Floating Market. I doubt whether any tourist saw a scene like this. My western, middle-class morality was hit for six. It took me a long time to recover, and I spent many hours trying to reconcile the irreconcilable.

My companions meanwhile, all except John, were coming round to my point of view that there was no commercial outcome to be had here, and were increasingly spending their time enjoying themselves, while John carried on grimly with endless meetings. Our hosts were still very obliging and made sure that we saw all the wonderful sights of the city. This included the royal palace, but we had no audience with the King and Queen. What happened to the corgis? We never found out. The cynical among us suggested that they had formed part of one of our delicious meals.

The time was rapidly approaching to go home. Thip and I had grown very close. On our last night, I bought her a gold chain that she liked, and a bottle of whisky. She said that she wanted to drown her sorrows, as she listened to the sound of my plane taking off. We did correspond for a time afterwards, but her English was not good enough, and she had her letters written for her, which removed the intimacy. She was saddened, she told me, by a Gaugin postcard that I sent her. I thought it was a rather good likeness, but she was not flattered.

5

KENYA

In the Footsteps of the Profligate Son

It was more a tale of the profligate son than the prodigal son. The proprietor of an extremely successful German tour operator, sending plane-loads of lower-end tourists to Kenya on a weekly basis, had decided to expand by buying hotels there. He had sent out his son, whom he was trying to integrate into the business, to spy out the land and make strategic purchases. The son had done as he was told, but also was drunk for the whole period of his stay. As a result, he could not remember what hotels he had bought. The son had been banished from the scene. As an English lawyer, I was being asked to go to Kenya to make discreet enquiries, ascertain what hotels the company owned, and report on them.

After my initial incredulity, it increasingly seemed an excellent idea. I arranged to take Maggie, my recently qualified assistant and future wife. I saw no reason why we should not turn the trip into an advance honeymoon. We flew to Frankfurt, where we joined the chartered tour plane. It was all non-stop jollity, making Butlin's seem like a church social. When we crossed the Equator, there was a replica of a ship ceremony, with a nearly naked Neptune racing up and down the aisle, beating the passengers over the head with an inflated club. They have a saying in East Africa: 'What is more dangerous? The angry elephant? The charging rhinoceros? No, it is to be caught between the advancing German tourists and the dining room when the dinner gong sounds!'

Our first stop was the Westwood Park, a somewhat run-down

country club in the hills outside Nairobi. The profligate son, before the drink took hold, recalled buying this establishment. This meant that I merely had to establish title, and the price paid through local lawyers, as well as make a written report on what needed to be done to bring the place up to the required standard. We were able to spend a few very pleasant days sunbathing and otherwise getting acclimatised.

Other clients, Indian traders, were kind enough to lend us a Toyota, which was parked on the edge of an extremely busy market. I am always a nervous starter with an unfamiliar car, and it was so positioned that my first movement would be in reverse, in the path of a group of young children, who insisted on playing in the dirt there. I had to use Maggie to continually shoo them away, and I had visions of starting our trip to Mombasa by running over one of them with disastrous results.

Our start was uneventful, but the road soon changed from smooth tarmac to red dust. This presented us with a dilemma. We could keep the windows shut, the dust out and swelter, or we could open the windows and be covered with red dust from head to foot. We chose the latter option, which necessitated long showers to get the dust out of ears, hair and other awkward places.

The countryside was getting wilder, and we were approaching the Tsavo Game Reserve. I was astonished that earth could be such a rich, red colour, far more so than the red earth of Cornwall. Huge anthills rising up from the flat plain were very strange to me, as were the baobab trees, which seemed to be planted upside down with roots where the leaves and branches should be. There were elephants grazing by the roadside, and Maggie issued a peremptory call to stop just as we passed one particularly hulking bull elephant. Before I could say a word, she was out of the car, camera at the ready, steadily approaching the grazing bull. I realised that she did not know the difference between wild African and tame Indian elephants. I kept the engine running with my feet on brake and accelerator simultaneously. The bull looked up to see Maggie, gave an angry snort and moved towards her. To her credit, she speedily grasped the situation and took off for the car. I held the door open for her as she jumped in. I accelerated as fast as I could but I was afraid of stalling the car. We gradually gained speed, and my eyes were fixed on the rear mirror, which was filled with an enraged elephant growing even larger. Gradually, it started to diminish in size, and we were safe. We were both shaken by the experience, and I begged her never to repeat it.

It was quickly getting dark, and we were nowhere near the lodge at Tsavo West where we were due to stay the night. I am used in England to cats' eyes on the road to aid navigation, but a string of cats' eyes crossing the road in front of us, caught in our headlights, was disconcerting. It was good to arrive at the lodge, which I felt was quite a triumph for such innocents abroad.

We reached the coast and headed south. Our work was now beginning with tactful enquiries of hotel managers as to who owned their establishment. Our experiences were uniformly good. We made a few 'hits', but even more 'misses'. Some of the information that we obtained was frightening. Pemba Island, owned by Tanzania, just off the southern tip of Kenya, was garrisoned by the Chinese, who had a missile base there. At whom were the missiles pointing? What was their range? This was not information that you picked up in the daily press. Various fishing boats and their crews, we were told, ventured too near the island, never to be seen again.

Mombasa was an exotic change of scenery. To eat spicy Indian vegetarian food out of a newspaper cone bought by the roadside was a novel experience. This city was an intriguing mixture of Indian and Arab influences, in contrast to Nairobi with its gleaming modern buildings and African slums.

Continuing our journey down the coast, we identified Whispering Palms, a delightful venue, as one of our hotels. We were sitting enjoying an early evening drink there at a small metal table beneath some of the whispering palms, when a coconut fell with a clang onto the table, creating considerable dent. If that had been a foot the other way, one of our skulls could have suffered greatly.

We learned from the owner of the Swordfish Hotel in Malindi

(not a target property), that he had difficulty recruiting Kenyan taxi drivers, as they could earn more money acting as male prostitutes for the German women tourists. AIDS was not a problem then, but I have little doubt that its spread into the heterosexual community was helped by this proclivity.

It was clear that our man had never reached Malindi, so we had no excuse to prolong the trip. The journey back at first seemed almost uneventful. I had a bad habit of running down the petrol tank, and it could be done quite scientifically there, as petrol stations were marked on the map. Once again, we were driving between the two Tsavo Game Reserves and it was getting near the end of the day. We reached the projected petrol station only to find that it was being re-built and no fuel was for sale. The next station was on the outskirts of Nairobi and a long way away with a nearly empty tank in an unfamiliar car. We realised how isolated this spot was. Whereas before there always seemed to be people trudging along beside the road, or just standing or squatting there, now there was nobody. So we continued our journey in suppressed panic. This was getting worse, as the fuel light started to flicker. The road was completely empty, and I was glad to see a coach parked by the road-side. I stopped to see if I could borrow or buy a can of petrol, only to find that the coach was abandoned with a big black streak and dent down the side. It looked as if it had had a far too close encounter with an elephant. I wondered if it was our elephant. It was just about the right spot. Perhaps he was still so angry at Maggie's approach that he took it out on the next vehicle to appear. We limped into Nairobi with the last few drops of fuel in the tank. I learned a valuable lesson.

My report on the hotels was long and detailed. I hope it helped the clients.

6

MAURITIUS

Everything but the Dodo

Humphry Berkeley was a paradoxical and ultimately infuriating character. He had been President of the Cambridge Union, and that normally is a passport at least to Cabinet rank. He had been elected at a very young age to Parliament, and there seemed no obstacle in his path to greatness, except his own temperament. Humphry was courageous to the point of foolhardiness. He alienated his very conservative constituents by his support of the abolition of capital punishment, and of the rights of homosexuals. He picked fights without thought or fear of the consequences. As a result, his career prospects descended. He was a very good client to have, and an ideal one for fostering my international travel ambitions. He had used his time in Parliament to make good contacts throughout the Commonwealth, and now was part of a brilliant team running a company with multifarious interests in various countries.

He was due to make a trip to Mauritius, and asked me to accompany him. It was agreed that Maggie would come as my assistant and we had a number of meetings to plan our business activities. Investico, Humphry's company, was backing a group of former high-level executives, who had been running a big fast food operation. They had formed a similar business entitled Beefy Bars, and wanted to open in Mauritius. Investico was also involved in the construction of a new hotel there to be called La Pirogue, after the shape of the canoe, which it was to resemble. It was thought that part of the cost could be raised by a local corporate flotation.

My experience of that type of work would reinforce the local knowledge of the Mauritian professionals.

Humphry was staying with friends, while we were at the Le Morne Hotel, very much a tourist establishment. We were served South African canned fruit and vegetables, which was ridiculous, as there was an abundance of first-rate produce to be found locally. After one trip to the market in Port Louis, the capital, we returned laden with beautiful fruit and vegetables, which we triumphantly took to the kitchen. From then on, we ate like kings.

The key word to describe Mauritius is diversity. It has been ruled by the Portuguese, the Dutch, the French and the British. All left their mark in one way or the other. Port Louis is particularly Portuguese. The legal profession, like Gaul according to Caesar, is divided into three parts: notaries after the French, and barristers and solicitors after the British. The population is even more mixed: whites of French and British origin, Indians, blacks imported to work in agriculture, and Chinese. Mauritian cuisine is particularly diverse with French, Indian and Chinese influences predominant. The terrain and climate are very varied, ranging from mountains with seemingly perpetual rain – they say it always rains in Curepipe, the island's second city – to fields of head-high waving sugar cane, where you have to climb onto the roof of your car to spot a land-mark. There are endless sand and coral beaches. We tried to explore them all.

The next day's business meeting was a strange affair. We were trying to sell the concept of the Beefy Bars franchise to a group of local investors. I had stayed up most of the night drafting a franchise agreement which was plagiarised from a Hertz Car Hire contract. For hire cars, substitute beef burgers! The potential investors were strangely reticent, and I was determined to find out the reason. It eventually transpired that they thought the name 'Beefy Bars' unmarketable in Mauritius, where forty per cent of the population were Hindus, to whom the cow was of course sacred! When I ironically suggested 'Dodobars' after the mystical but extinct local bird as an alternative, I was not met with a positive response. It proves that it pays to do your local homework.

Putting together the prospectus for the share issue for La Pirogue proved more successful. I was working with a local notaire, whose name, unlike mine, appeared on the prospectus, even though I was probably responsible for drafting most of the contents. He was from one of the old French families and extremely proud of it. After a hard day's work and a lot to drink, he shattered my ideas of racial harmony, which I thought existed in the island. I had to keep quiet for the sake of the project, but it was difficult.

We seemed in many respects to be living in the Wild West, as there were no securities or consumer protection laws. You could say what you liked, true or not. Our prospectus was more like an advertisement. Being accustomed to the detailed restrictions of the City of London, it was a culture shock to find out how liberated we were. The prospectus looked good, when it was published in the local paper, and ran for three days. I was however completely nonplussed when the request came to translate the prospectus into Mandarin Chinese, as it was felt that their community always liked a gamble, and their English language skills were lacking. It was done, but I took no responsibility for its accuracy or otherwise. The money rolled in from all sides, and the hotel was built. I hope to go back one day, before they pull it down, and see what I helped to accomplish.

Humphry was very well connected in Mauritius and introduced us to an exotic variety of local characters, ranging from rich local Indians, many of whom had beautiful, model-style French wives, to the Foreign Minister, Gaetan Duval, who wore exotic Pierre Cardin suits and was extremely camp. The thought of him prancing down the stuffy corridors of Whitehall brought a smile to my face. Mauritius should be on everybody's travel agenda, but try and get off the tourist track.

7

KENYA RE-VISITED

Exploring the Coffee Bean Trail

It did not seem a promising situation. I had known R.H. Shah for some time. He ran various retail businesses including a newsagents in Greenwich. He had achieved media notoriety a few years before by sending some of his paper boys and girls as a special reward on trips to Kenya. They had been asked to bring back 'gifts' for friends, and those parcels had very much interested HM Customs on their return. I had acted for him in achieving the release from Customs of a consignment of Kenyan wooden curios. The curios themselves were not of interest, but the packaging, which consisted of British banknotes of various denominations, certainly was. Customs moved to impound the lot, until I read in the appropriate Act that they could impound goods, but goods did not include currency. I facetiously offered to let them keep the wooden curios, but Mr Shah was able to collect the whole consignment. This was of course long before the advent of money laundering as a crime. In those days, one country's tax and exchange control laws were perceived as another country's opportunity.

The story Mr Shah now told me sounded very far fetched. The failure that year of the coffee crop in South America meant that the value of the East African crop was sky high. A fine example of one man's loss being another man's gain. He was part of a consortium which had acquired a large consignment of top-class coffee beans, or 'black gold', as it was known colloquially. The consignment had originated in the Congo and had gradually found its way to the port of Mombasa from where it had been shipped to Amsterdam, where it had been wrongly, so it was said, impounded by a large Belgian commodity house, which claimed ownership.

He produced copies of a sheaf of affidavits and supporting documents, all of which proved that the Belgian company had no title. He told me that they were all false, and had been obtained as a result of bribery and other forms of corruption. I guessed that Mr Shah had fallen out with other members of his syndicate and now wished to change sides. He felt that my powers of advocacy were such that I would be able to persuade the Belgian company to fund my expedition to East Africa to ferret out the truth and obtain counter evidence, which would enable them to prove ownership in Amsterdam and dispose of the coffee. He was prepared to finance my trip with him to the company's headquarters in Antwerp to that end.

I had no great confidence in my powers of persuasion, but I went along for the ride, as it were. Surprisingly, we were successful and the company announced that it was prepared to instruct me, and pay my fees and expenses, to go out to East Africa to collect the evidence. Mr Shah's reward was to be a share of the proceeds of the coffee once released. Uganda was the obvious place for me to start but Idi Amin thought otherwise, as British citizens were unwelcome there at the time. Mr Shah assured me that this was no obstacle, as all the witnesses would be prepared to travel to Kenya to meet me. I thought it best at this stage not to ask the obvious question as to why people who had been bribed to give testimony one way should suddenly be prepared to put themselves to great inconvenience to contradict themselves, for no obvious reward, and now give testimony the other way.

I was asked where I would like to interview the witnesses. I replied, facetiously, 'At the poolside of the Intercontinental in Nairobi.' I was told that it would be arranged. It is not surprising that the many handwritten pages of witnesses' testimony, obtained as a result of the trip, had a strong whiff of Ambre Solaire.

Once again, it was agreed that Maggie would accompany me and we prepared ourselves for a very busy trip. Establishing the chain of events was fascinating. The coffee, a mixture of arabica and robusta beans, originated in the Congo under respectable ownership. It had been bagged and shipped for ultimate consignment by lorry to Mombasa. A gang of Somali villains, recruited specially for the purpose, had ambushed the convoy of lorries in Uganda. The coffee had been taken to a secret depot, where it had been mixed with Ugandan coffee of good quality, re-bagged and a new set of title documents, all of course false, provided. During my interviews, I was given a complete set of pro-forma official-looking documents and false government seals as evidence. The coffee was then re-loaded on the original lorries, which were provided with fake number plates and documentation. The convoy then made its way to Mombasa under the care of the Somalis, with one of them 'riding shotgun' in the cabin of each lorry, as there was fear that there would be a further hijacking. From there, the coffee made its way by ship to Amsterdam, only to be impounded by the company, the rightful owners – or were they?

As we sat by the pool of the Intercontinental enjoying the sun, a very mixed bag of characters was paraded before us. These included senior Customs officials, border guards, traders, drivers, coffee farmers and obvious rogues. We had their original affidavits before us, and they now, with absolutely no apology, told the completely opposite story. A happy week passed and we improved our suntans immeasurably. One memorable evening, we found ourselves as one of the only two couples on the dance floor in the night club at the Intercontinental. The other man was Muhammad Ali, who was then President Jimmy Carter's informal ambassador to Africa. He was dressed in an extremely smart white suit and to be near him on the dance floor was an awe-inspiring experience. He was not only huge, but gave off an aura of enormous power.

Armed with our wad of affidavits and exhibits, we made our return journey to the company's office in Antwerp. They were pleased at what we had to give them. Both sides' evidence was completely contradictory, and there was now sufficient doubt for the company to be able to effect a compromise deal, and have the coffee released and sold. From the smile on Mr Shah's face, I had a feeling that he had benefited from both sides. It was in keeping with the total ambivalence of the whole enterprise.

8

TRANSKEI

Country of Barely Concealed Menace

Humphry Berkeley came up with an interesting trip yet again. He announced that he had been appointed diplomatic representative of the government of Transkei. When I looked blank, he told me that Transkei was one of a number of so-called 'Homelands', established by the pro-apartheid government of South Africa to show the world that it was prepared to let the black people have self-government in certain areas. Humphry was a vociferous opponent of apartheid, and I wondered whether Transkei had made a wise choice in his appointment, as it was clear that the new country, landlocked and surrounded on all sides by South Africa, needed to keep good relations with its parent.

Humphry wanted Maggie and me to accompany him on a trip to Transkei, where we would be appointed lawyers to the government, and there would be all sorts of interesting business opportunities. The fact that our trip was to be funded by Transkei undoubtedly influenced my acceptance.

We flew to Johannesburg, and I have to say that I found the evidence of apartheid all around us an unacceptable shock. Buses, hotels, restaurants and bars, if they allowed admittance to blacks at all, had segregated areas for them. It was hard to accept that this was a way of life.

Humphry gleefully told us – he loved making mischief – that he had been in contact with the government of Nigeria, and that he had in his briefcase a proposal for the Nigerian army to take over the training of the Transkei army. I had to avoid looking at Maggie, as we both knew we were treading on very dangerous ground. Apart from going by road, the only way of getting to Transkei was by the South African-owned airline. It soon became apparent that South Africa controlled all communications, and all external activities, of Transkei.

We were on the flight to Umtata, Transkei's capital, when Humphry suddenly realised that he was without his briefcase. He had left it at Johannesburg Airport, he thought. I had a much more sinister interpretation. I reckoned that it had been stolen by BOSS, the South African secret service. Humphry was so naturally indiscreet, that he had broadcast his views on apartheid to all and sundry. I assumed that BOSS now held the secret plans for training the Transkei army. I did not feel at all happy about the situation. We never did find out what happened to the briefcase.

Umtata was run-down, desolate and cold. We were staying in the Holiday Inn, the only half decent hotel in the place. I was not encouraged by the sight of the empty swimming pool – shades of Graham Greene's *The Comedians*. The next day, we were taken to meet President Kaiser Matanzima, and his brother, George, the Prime Minister. Our trip was due to last three days, and I was keen to get started on business discussions as soon as possible. Clearly, they did not share my concern, as we were dispatched back to our hotel with nothing to do, and nothing achieved.

This continued for three days, and I decided that we had to cut our losses and leave. I asked for another audience with the President, and told him that we wished to leave. His response was that he wished us to stay. As he controlled the means of exit, his wish was equivalent to a command. There were all sorts of political shifts and changes taking place, which we did not understand. Breakfast in the hotel restaurant was the daily key to how we were viewed in high places. If those present acknowledged us and smiled at us, it was a good day. However, if they ignored us and turned their backs on us, the converse applied.

At the weekend, we were invited by the Finance Minister, who had been a lecturer in economics at Ealing Technical College, to attend his son's coming of age celebration at their country home. Probing a little deeper, we learned that Transkei males at the age of eighteen were ritually circumcised by the local witch doctor. They had to spend the night in vigil in the open before the celebrations the next day. Having learned from his experience in the West, his son was being circumcised by a doctor, but the other boys in the group were having it done the traditional way.

I felt as if we were stepping into the pages of the *National Geographic* magazine. The boys were huddled in a group, dressed in blankets with white paint on their faces. It looked as if they were in shock after a very unpleasant operation, which was hardly surprising. The women were dancing vigorously and uttering weird and disturbing shouts. One of them came over to the three of us, the only Europeans at the ceremony, with a tray of slippery-looking stuff. It was explained to us that this was raw tripe, or cow's stomach lining, a special delicacy served on this occasion. I watched Maggie's and Humphry's faces turning green. There was clearly no way that they would be able to touch the stuff. The honour of England was now on my slender shoulders. I managed to eat a portion and a half to show my appreciation, but then the acrid farmyard smell became too much even for me. I could only do so much for England.

The days kept passing with no obvious change in our situation. We were effectively prisoners at the mercy of the Matanzima brothers, who were living like kings. The people of Transkei existed on subsistence agriculture and money sent back by the young men, who went to work in terrible conditions in the South African mines. They lived packed close together in barracks while they were working in the mines, and their ambition was to save up enough to buy a wife, a cow and a patch of land to work. The Matanzimas, by contrast, lived in large houses, and were ferried around in air-conditioned Mercedes limousines. South Africa had bought them and kept the whole country under strict control. The aura of independence was a complete sham designed to fool the rest of the world that enlightened changes were taking place. My first-hand view was very disillusioning.

After ten days of virtual imprisonment, we were summoned suddenly again before the President. He had a list of instructions for me including my firm's appointment as the government's lawyers. We were to leave the next day. The timing of the instructions meant that we would have to hit the ground running on our return to London. I suggested that we upgrade our flights to first class accordingly at the government's expense , and this was accepted.

We were flying South African Airways, and at the time the black African countries would not allow SAA to fly over their territory. As a result, we had to fly over the Atlantic, and refuel at Isla da Sal in the Cape Verde Islands. We landed at night on what was little more than a large billiard table buffeted by constant winds.

The main aftermath of the trip was predictably unpleasant. I have already referred to the atmosphere of menace, which was almost palpable. Humphrey stayed on, when Maggie and I left. I could never decide whether he was extremely brave or very fool-hardy, or perhaps he was insensitive to the risks he was running. He was abducted one day, shoved into the boot of a car and taken out into the country, where he was beaten up and left for dead by the side of the road. He was fortunate enough to be rescued and survived the experience.

My own aftermath was physically painless, though financially damaging. I submitted my bill to the government, but they failed to pay it. I sent various reminders, but there was no response. Eventually, I asked local lawyers to sue for recovery. I had overlooked the fact that the action would have to take place in the government's courts, and what this meant in a corrupt society. At a preliminary hearing I was ordered to deposit three times the amount of the claim on account of the government's costs before I could continue with the action. The time had come to cut my losses and run. In retrospect, I recognised that for a fleetingly short time we were *honorary* lawyers to the government of Transkei. It was hardly worth a mention in the firm's formal history.

9

ST KITTS

The Dark Secret of a Sunny Island

Rosemary Berkeley was Humphry's half sister. Her mother, Gladys, had been the grande dame of St Kitts, owing her position in society to the family sugar plantation. Rosemary had not enjoyed a close relationship with her mother, but there had been a sudden rapprochement as her mother mellowed with age. She had told Rosemary that she was the beneficiary under her Will, although she still discouraged her daughter from visiting the island. You can imagine Rosemary's shock, when she heard of her mother's death well into her nineties, and that she had inherited nothing. Everything was left to the estate's black overseer, Joseph. However, Joseph did not enjoy his fortune for long. He died suddenly, and his widow, the family cook, inherited the money, the mansion, the plantation and all the contents.

Rosemary asked me what could be done. I explained that her mother might have lacked the mental or physical capacity to make a valid Will at that late stage in her life. It was possible that her servants had exercised undue influence, or even duress, in ensuring that Mrs Berkeley changed her Will in her overseer's favour to the exclusion of her only child. The best way to find out was to conduct an investigation locally and Humphry urged her to send me to conduct it. I agreed to go over during the Christmas holidays with Maggie. I said that I wanted our travelling and hotel expenses paid, but I accepted the principle of a reduced fee, as we planned to have a holiday at the same time.

I divide West Indian Islands into two categories: those that have airports where large jets can land – these tend to be overrun with American tourists and the US dollar reigns supreme – and those where you have to change onto a much smaller plane to get there, which tend to retain a more individual identity. We were happy to find that St Kitts fell into the latter category. Our hotel was delightful, with individual bungalows. We settled in well, but I was perturbed to find a scruffy note in a badly hand-written envelope the next morning, which had been pushed under the door. The message was short: 'We know why you are here. If you know what's good for you, leave the island now, or you will be cut up into little pieces.' The note was of course unsigned. We debated whether to call the police, but eventually decided, perhaps stupidly, to ignore it, although we became much more wary of strangers, especially black ones, as at least the original source of the note was fairly obvious.

Our enquiries caused us to meet a wide variety of people on the island. It was a particularly stratified society, each part with its own clubs and activities. There seemed to be little cross-traffic. As outsiders and fresh faces, we seemed to be welcome across the board. There were the old whites, who consisted of the sugar barons, and their professional advisers. The new whites were mainly from the big UK contractors on short-term assignments with their families. I felt sorry for the coloureds, those of mixed race, who seemed to sit uneasily in the middle, although they comprised the bulk of the professional and commercial people, who actually ran the economy. They all seemed to have a big chip on their shoulder. The blacks were in certain respects at the bottom of the pile, except that they ran the island politically.

As we were in the West Indies, I felt it obligatory to see some cricket. The match was St Kitts against the Leeward Islands. Unfortunately, it was the only day we were there that it rained. The ground staff came out to mop up and roll the pitch. They were a motley crew with US Marine-style haircuts and were wearing floppy canvas clothes. I asked one of our neighbours in the stand about them, and I was told that they were convicts from the local prison.

At first, I thought about the ease of escape. But where could they go? The island of Nevis was in sight, but the sea looked inhospitable and it was a long swim.

Everywhere you went on St Kitts, you heard the sound of steel band music. It was not a form of music that had particularly appealed to me before, but here it grew on you. I learned that they were practising for the Christmas competition. Each band was sponsored, and we sat through the whole day. The final was fought out between the Esso Band and the Coca-Cola Band. To this day, I can still hear in my head the plaintive strains of the theme from the Alamo, the Esso Band's winner, beaten out on steel drums of all shapes and sizes.

Our hotel was good, but there were even better ones tucked away inaccessibly in other parts of the island. The holy of holies, which attracted reclusive millionaires, was Cockleshell Bay. You could only reach it by small rowing boat, and the amenities did not include electricity. There seemed to be a reverse snobbery at work, where the less you got, the more you paid. The year ended with Carnival. Maggie was a compulsive photographer, but she reckoned without the unwillingness of the local population to be photographed. Whether this was due to superstition, or not, I do not know, but having ignored warning signs, she eventually had her camera dashed from her hands. That note apart, this was the only overt hostility that we met on the island.

As we investigated, the story was not at all what I had hoped to find. We found that everybody was happy to talk to us. We met Mrs Berkeley's doctors, her bank manager and her priest. They all told the same story. Even in her nineties and with certain physical frailties, her mental capacity never lessened. 'She was sharp as a tack,' as her bank manager put it. They laughed at the suggestion of duress or undue influence. It seemed that she tyrannised her neighbours and her servants especially, but I felt that they were all keeping something back.

Eventually the true story unfolded late one night in a smoky bar from an over-talkative bartender. The main reason that Mrs

Berkeley discouraged Rosemary from visiting the island was that she did not want her to know that the overseer, Joseph, was her lover and shared her bed. She always planned to leave her estate to him as a reward for all the services that he had rendered to her. The situation changed when Joseph suddenly and unexpectedly announced that he had married Sarah, the family cook. Mrs Berkeley threw him out of her bed, made a new Will making Rosemary her beneficiary, and generally restored the links with her daughter.

However, her anger against Joseph did not last and, despite his marriage to Sarah, he was reinstated as Mrs Berkeley's lover, and a new Will was made restoring him as beneficiary. I have to say that I fantasised at the physical strength as well as the mental capacity of a woman well into her nineties who could live such a dominant and active existence. Perhaps it was the vitamins in the sugar cane!

We enjoyed a wonderful holiday, but on our return we had bad news for our client. I tried to keep the true nature of the relationship between Mrs Berkeley and Joseph from Rosemary, but she guessed that too. As is so often the case, when the news is bad, the messenger gets shot. She refused to pay the balance of our bill, and left the country. I had certain sympathy for her and did not try too hard to find her. Humphry, ever the mischief-maker, was of course no help in that respect.

10

NASSAU

The Decline and Fall of an Empire

I was getting a reputation as the divorce lawyer of choice. This was only partly deserved. I had no interest in divorce law itself, and I found the squabbles over children distressing. I would wake in the middle of the night worrying about my clients' children, then contrast this with the fact that I lost no sleep over my own. Where I did score was by applying the principles of commercial negotiation to the division of assets and income, and apart from a few notable failures, this emphasis resolved many previously intractable situations. Recommendations were coming in from all sides. One of the most colourful was Martica Clapp. Born in poverty in Cuba, she had made her living initially as a diver.

She had then been drawn into the network of all talents employed by Investors Overseas Services (IOS), the worldwide financial group founded by Bernie Cornfeld originally to help US servicemen in Germany invest their surplus income. Martica had met and married Samuel Clapp, a very tall and dry Boston lawyer, who had also become part of the IOS world. It was an attraction of complete opposites, where the attraction soon faded, but not before they had built together a beautiful house in the Bahamas.

Sam had installed Linda Blanford, an upmarket English journalist, in their home and Martica wanted retribution and divorce as well. The problem was that there was no jurisdiction in England, and the petition would have to be issued in the Bahamas. I contacted Colin Callendar, a lawyer in Nassau who had helped me in the past. He told me that Martica would have to come out there to swear to the truth of the facts in her petition. She flatly refused to go, unless I accompanied her. Never one to turn down a trip, I made the arrangements.

The drive down Bay Street is always an event. There are so many buildings in the colonial style, completely covered with brass plates representing the many companies which have their registered offices there. We arrived just as the sun reached a certain angle, and its light on the brass plates was dazzling. We were stuck in the usual traffic jam by a platform, on which a tall Bahamian police woman in an extremely short skirt was trying to get the traffic moving. I had an almost irresistible urge to lean out of the car window and slide my hand up her leg and under that skirt. In a bar a few days later, I learned that this was a national sport and some of the participants were currently languishing in jail.

We were booked into the Royal Victoria Hotel, which was set in superb tropical gardens, and looked like something out of *Gone with the Wind*. I later learned that it was built during the American Civil War to house the blockade runners, who frequented Nassau at the time. I was shown to my room, opened the French windows, and stepped out onto the wooden balcony. It was a mistake. The balcony dipped, swayed and groaned alarmingly. I stepped back hastily. The hotel, picturesque relic that it was, was on its last legs. It had been demolished the next time I visited the island.

I took Martica to see Colin the next morning to swear the petition, and then straight to the airport. She could not wait to get out of the place, which had now such bad memories for her. After seeing her off at Departures, I slipped over to Arrivals to meet Maggie, who was on the incoming plane. I was staying on not only to supervise the service of the petition, but also to enjoy an illicit weekend with her. I think the reception staff at the Royal Victoria were a little confused. Martica had checked out of her room a few hours before, and now I was returning with Maggie to share my room. I think they thought it was the same woman. We had had a quarrel, then made it up, and decided to get much closer.

The next morning, we met the bailiff very early at the dockside, and chugged across the water to Paradise Island in his small boat. Paradise Island had originally been called Hog Island, and must have been a dismal place, until it was developed and re-named by Huntingdon Hartford, a very rich American. We were heading for the Dock House on the Clapp Estate, where Sam and Linda were supposed to be sleeping. When Martica first instructed me, she talked in her thick Cuban-American accent, as I thought, about the 'Dog House'. I thought it apt, but at the same time inappropriate as a name, and I was a little disappointed subsequently to discover the more prosaic, if more descriptive, epithet.

We landed, and stealthily approached the door to the house, which was unlocked. We climbed the wooden stairs directly into a large bedroom with a sloping ceiling. A shape arose in the gloom from the tangled covers on the large bed. 'Are you Samuel Clapp?' I asked. He answered affirmatively, so the bailiff handed him his papers. A smaller, more tousled, shape then also arose from the bed. 'Are you Linda Blandford?' I asked. She nodded, and the bailiff gave her her copy of the petition as well. Having had the advantage of surprise, we thought it best to make a quick getaway. The bailiff dropped us off at the other end of the beach, and we enjoyed the morning there. Maggie was wearing an extremely skimpy, but fashionable, yellow bikini, with a very distinctive sunflower pattern, which she had bought in the King's Road.

About noon, we decided to go for a walk along the beach. There in the distance coming towards us was a couple hand in hand with two huge dogs. The man was very tall, and the woman quite short. As they got nearer, I realised that it was Sam Clapp and Linda Blandford. The dogs were even bigger than I had thought, and looked like killers. I would have liked to have turned back, but it was tactically inappropriate. 'Oh my God,' I said to Maggie out of the side of my mouth, 'I think we are going to be lunch!' I then realised that Linda was wearing exactly the same exclusive bikini as Maggie. To find two women on a beach in the same outfit in these difficult circumstances was doubly embarrassing, especially as we were looking at the type of one-off design where, in my innocence, I assumed that the creator, having produced the original, was immediately taken out and shot. The price paid for the skimpy garments would have justified such a course of action, and also paid for an expensive funeral.

'We thought you might be here,' Sam said, 'so we came to invite you back for lunch.' I was flabbergasted, but could only nod agreement. We walked back together, and they made small talk. It was a pity we had not come the day before, as there had been a marvellous party. The survivors were still there, and they were sure we would love to meet them. The scene which met our eyes as we walked onto the large, stone-flagged terrace overlooking the sea, with huge terra cotta vases containing exotic trailing plants everywhere, was like something out of a Bacchanalian orgy. There were chaises set out all over the place, most of which were occupied by paunchy, unhealthy-looking New York stockbroker types, dressed only in Bermuda shorts, and being serviced in various ways by myriads of beautiful, sunburned girls dressed in bikinis.

I recognised the actor, Laurence Harvey, and the couturier, Oleg Cassini. Bernie Cornfeld himself looked like the Emperor Nero with his balding tonsure. He was surrounded by three girls, one of whom was dropping grapes from a height into his open mouth. I lay down weakly on an empty chaise beside a beautiful bronzed girl in a pink bikini. 'My name is Amanda McCall. I'm one of the McCalls, and I'll have you know I'm not Bernie Cornfeld's hooker,' was how she opened the conversation. I replied politely: 'My dear, I never thought for one moment that you were.'

I was feeling increasingly sorry for Martica, whom, I knew, had spent so much time and effort planning and building this beautiful place, only to see it taken over by this sybaritic mob. Despite the wonderful food and wines, it was no hardship to leave and go back to the hotel to collect our bags, before going on to the airport.

Martica did get some revenge. About a week later she invited us out to the Arethusa in Chelsea, a very fashionable restaurant. She was accompanied by a tall, young, extremely handsome would-be actor named Peter Lawrence. When the time to pay the bill arrived, I was very amused to see the surreptitious transfer under cover of the tablecloth of a wad of bank notes from Martica to Peter, so that he could be seen to pay it. She was extremely good to Peter, and sent him to the method acting school in New York run by Lee Strasberg. The peak of Peter's acting career was the second lead to Oliver Tobias in one of Joan Collins' films, *The Stud*. He then became a successful property developer.

Sadly, I do not think that Martica ever regained the heady heights and grand position of life in the giddy whirl of IOS that she had once enjoyed. She was a casualty of divorce and of the system, although, when IOS finally collapsed, she would probably have lost her fortune anyway. Hers was the life of a shooting star.

11

SINGAPORE

The Sinister Side of Dictatorship

Brian Wein was in many ways the perfect client. He was an imaginative entrepreneur, who was always making things happen. His true strength was in sales and marketing, but, like so many of that type, he saw himself wrongly as a manager too. He relied on me for commercial as well as legal advice, and I was in effect an informal board member. His communications group was growing extremely fast, and offices were being opened throughout the world. It reached the point where he wanted to float on the London Stock Exchange. With misgivings that I will explain shortly, I introduced him to a stockbroker, in the expectation that the proposal would swiftly be killed, but I was surprised to find that the broker was extremely keen, and I was asked to put in place the usual apparatus for a public issue.

The problem, which nobody except me seemed to appreciate, was that many of the group's activities were technically illegal, as they offended the monopoly of local state telecommunication organisations. There was little point in debating the rights and wrongs of such laws. They were an example of naked state protectionism, but they made many of the group's activities hazardous, and the risk of being shut down locally was always present.

Having given many warnings of the risk, Cassandra-like, it gave me little pleasure to be proved right, when I was told that the Commercial Crime Squad had swooped on the group's offices in Singapore, arrested the local manager and impounded all the communications equipment. I had worked with Singapore lawyers before, so I knew about the regime's shoot first and ask questions afterwards policy. I had been involved in one case where every time we wanted a document, our counterpart local law firm had to ask the police specifically to release it, as all their files had been confiscated. If it was only inanimate objects that were at risk, I would not have been so worried, but I knew that the government also had a habit of imprisoning lawyers and accountants without trial, not to mention company directors.

I advised Brian that the local directors, who fortunately were out of Singapore at the time, were at great risk if they returned. I was shocked when he then asked me to fly out and sort out the mess. My first thought, I had to admit, was for my own safety. From reading Russell Braddon, I was well aware of the reputation of Changi Jail during the war, and I did not fancy a fact-finding mission to ascertain whether it had improved afterwards.

I said that I would only go if I could first negotiate my safe conduct. My friend from Cambridge days, Joe Grimberg, was senior partner of Drew & Napier, one of the best law firms there, and I asked him for help. It was only when I received an assurance that I committed to the trip. I was very busy at the time and, much as the idea appealed, I could not turn my visit into a quasi-holiday. It was a question of a swift trip there and back, so I insisted on first-class travel. Having to judge between the merits of British Airways out and Singapore Airlines back was a difficult but pleasant task. Singapore won on points.

On arriving, I went straight into a meeting with the police to try to resolve the situation. Sachi Saurajen, one of the Drew & Napier partners, accompanied me. The contrast between the office occupied by the police and the offices of the local law firms was extraordinary. The law firms all seemed to operate out of magnificent glass and marble palaces with views of the harbour, while the police occupied dirty, dingy premises without air conditioning, and with old and chipped office furniture. Singapore is a steamy place, and a few lazily turning fans suspended from the ceiling did little to ease my sense of total displacement and jet lag.

I had persuaded Brian, much against his will, that we had to be seen to abandon our Singapore operations if we were to be able to wriggle out of a sticky situation, and if the public issue was to continue. The best that we could hope for was that we could recover and re-export our valuable equipment, secure the release from prison of the local manager and persuade the police not to bring a prosecution, especially if the company was prepared to make a voluntary contribution to State funds without any admission of guilt. Surprisingly, my proposals were quite well received. Police the world over relish an easy victory, and Singapore was no exception. We left the meeting without a deal, but with the likelihood that there would be one, especially if the voluntary contribution was quite generous.

We went back to Sachi's office, where I took a call from one of the local directors. He wanted to convene a board meeting that same evening in Kuala Lumpur in Malaysia to consider the situation. Sachi and I hopped on a local flight, and we checked into the Hilton. By now, I was so disorientated that one more flight hardly mattered. I repeated my advice that it was unsafe for the directors to return to Singapore, until a deal was done, and managed to get quite a good night's sleep.

The next morning, we flew back to Singapore for a further meeting with the police. They do not waste much time there, and I was extremely impressed that they were prepared to do the deal. Sachi and I drafted the paperwork, and, as I was carrying the client's power of attorney, I was able to sign it on the company's behalf. A government official was produced, who signed on behalf of the State, and we walked out into the bright light and clammy heat, in time for a celebratory lunch.

After that, Sachi went back to his office, and I was left to kill time before the evening flight back to London. By then, I was feeling desperately tired. I saw a Hyatt hotel opposite, and on the spur of the moment checked in for a few hours' sleep. I think the desk clerk was surprised to see a man checking in on his own for a few hours after a very good lunch, instead of the usual furtive couple with more obvious intentions. Including travelling time, I was away for little more than forty-eight hours, but I reckoned without the after-effects of such a trip. It was more than two weeks before I was fully functional again.

It was always a pleasure to act for clients like Brian Wein, who had so much confidence in my ability to perform without constant supervision or interference. Somehow, if you are sufficiently trusted, you grow in ability and perform the larger role that the client requires. I wish that all clients were like him.

12

INDIAN AND OTHER WEDDINGS

A Fantasy World of Luxury

I nearly always had a substantial number of Indian clients. I generalise, but it was a regular occurrence to be treated as one of the family by them. This included being invited to weddings. It was often ideal, like the Kennedys in their presidential years, although for different reasons, to eat something first, as dinner, although delicious when it eventually came, was often very much delayed. At the top of the market, these weddings had many aspects of Hollywood about them. There was a great spirit of competition at work. One family would employ minor royalty as the wedding planner. At the next event, the Lester Lanin Ballroom Orchestra would be flown in for the night from New York. I did gently suggest that there were some pretty good dance bands here, but I missed the point.

At one magnificent event at the Dorchester in Park Lane, the first sight to greet guests was an enormous ice sculpture of a swan. I watched it through the evening, melting away gently, rather like the host of the evening's bank balance. At the same wedding, during a superb buffet meal, there were no less than three cabarets. The last consisted of extraordinary dancers. I complimented the host, who happened to pass by, on their quality. 'They should be good,' he groaned. 'They are costing me an arm and a leg. It's the chorus of the Bolshoi Ballet.' At another wedding in an affluent North London suburb, the neighbours were astonished to see the

61

groom arriving on a white horse in the true Punjabi fashion.

Best of all though, were the weddings in India. To receive an invitation to one of those was a special mark of esteem, as the costs involved were huge. It goes without saying that free first-class flights were provided. A chauffeur-driven limousine met you at the airport, and was available for your every whim throughout the duration of the wedding, and luxurious hotel accommodation was also of course part of the package.

The first wedding I attended of this type was like an initiation rite. Maggie and I were met at Bombay Airport in the early hours of the morning by the groom's brother, and the obligatory chauffeur-driven, air-conditioned Mercedes, which was ours for the duration. We drove through the slums into the centre of town. The windows of the car were shut tight, so we could not experience the noxious aromas that must be arising, but the sights were bad enough. Those homes built with corrugated iron sheeting were veritable palaces by contrast to those built out of cardboard boxes clearly showing their origins as containers for various items of white goods. The poor devils living in them were lucky compared with the many who just rolled themselves in a blanket and slept by the roadside. It was light by now and, as we approached the centre of town, I was amazed to see young boys, properly clad in whites, practising in the cricket nets on various parched dry sports fields. I realised that they needed to get in their practice then, before the heat of the day made such energetic movements intolerable.

We arrived at the Oberoi Hotel, and were shown up to our suite on the twenty-ninth floor. We had incredible panoramic views of the city, only spoilt by the smog that covered the place like a blanket. We had a corner suite, and the lounge was big enough for five-a-side football. So far as the car and driver were concerned, when not actually shuttling between hotels for the various wedding events, we wanted to have as much rest as possible, in order to be well equipped for the fray. We, therefore, had no need of the car, and I once told the driver that he could take time off. This was clearly the wrong thing to do, as he told me – gently, but firmly. He was engaged to drive us, and nothing could deflect him from that purpose. If we did not require his services at that particular moment, we might suddenly need them on a whim, and therefore he must wait with the other drivers, just in case we changed our minds. He was as difficult to shift as chewing gum on the sole of your shoe.

The next five days flashed past in non-stop entertainment. The groom's and the bride's families were in competition to see who could put on the more lavish and spectacular events. The best singers and dancers in India were provided for our entertainment. Needless to say, the food and drink were magnificent. We did manage some time at the side of the pool, and I had a wonderful massage in coconut oil, although I ended up smelling like a Lyons cupcake. I always wondered about the length of a Sikh's hair, as it is never cut. In the poolside locker room my curiosity was at last satisfied, as I saw a young man freshly out of the shower with his hair extending below his knees.

After four days, the actual wedding took place on the fifth day. The Crystal Room of the Taj Mahal Hotel was banked with the most beautiful flowers. There were at least five thousand people present. The combined effect of people and flowers was too much for the air conditioning system, which packed up completely. We were sweltering, and there was no let up as the Hindu ceremony with its monotone chanting went on endlessly. I understood why Indians are so good in cricket at five-day test matches. It is something to do with the nature of their religion and the endless patience required.

I felt sorry for the bride and groom who had to sit there throughout the interminable proceedings on their beautifully carved thrones, dressed in traditional and extremely heavy looking, jewel-encrusted robes, while five thousand guests filed past to congratulate them. I realised that the wedding was for the benefit of the families, rather than the happy couple, who would have to wait their turn to get the full benefit, when their own children were eventually married. In fact the wedding invitation itself resembled a corporate merger document. Not only were the families listed at the top, but the names of all the companies that they controlled.

Before leaving for London, we took time to visit another client in Bombay, a textile manufacturer. His apartment was the ground floor of a former Maharajah's palace. There were servants everywhere. We had drinks, and then he told me that we were going to a wedding reception. I protested, as we had no invitation. He said that an invitation was unnecessary, and I would know people there. Strangely enough, he was right, as there was a lawyer there with whom I had done business.

When the time came to leave for the wedding, he stood up and clapped his hands. A servant came forward and knelt before him. The client put his hand on the servant's shoulder, who removed his slippers and replaced them with shoes. He caught me watching this operation. After all, he had an MBA from Harvard, and must be capable of putting on his own shoes. In the car, he explained. 'He has put on my shoes since I was a small child. His father put on my father's shoes, and his grandfather my grandfather's. We support eleven members of the family. I, of course, am perfectly capable of putting on my own shoes.' I then asked him how many servants he had. 'Sixteen in the apartment here, but about a hundred in our house near Delhi, including nurserymen and gardeners.' He then told me briefly about the social and economic structure of India. 'There are a million and a half to two million rich people. A growing middle class of one hundred and fifty to two hundred million, who are hungry to buy branded consumer goods, particularly from abroad, and the rest you can forget.' I found these last words chilling. To write off almost eight hundred million people on the sub-continent as having no hope was something I found hard to accept.

If I thought the first Bombay wedding was lavish, it was nothing compared with the next one. Many of the same rituals were followed. This time, I stayed at the Taj Mahal Hotel in Bombay, where a whole wing had been set aside for the wedding guests. There was a special hospitality desk which was open around the clock. Beset by jet lag at four in the morning, I was tempted to ring down and ask for an elephant sandwich. I am fairly confident that it would have been provided.

The groom's family was from Rajastan, and they wanted to preserve their tribal traditions. On the first evening I was invited to a so-called 'small and intimate' family gathering. This turned out to be a dinner for six hundred and fifty people, served on superbly engraved and chased silver plates. The actual wedding itself took place in the open air within the confines of a specially constructed replica of a seventeenth-century Rajastani fortress, with motionless sepoys holding muskets standing guard in the towers at the four corners. Before we reached there, we were all dressed in Rajastani turbans and processed along the Bombay waterfront, with the watching crowds held back by lines of police. The procession was led by an elephant covered in gold cloth and jewels. We were accompanied by dancers, acrobats, fire-eaters and sword swallowers, and the groom's grandfather's Rolls-Royce brought up the rear completely covered in a most intricate arrangement of small, white, jasmine-like flowers. I felt like Queen Victoria at a durbar to celebrate her diamond jubilee.

After five days of non-stop entertainment, I was ready to leave. I had actually converted the return half of my first-class ticket into an economy flight to Harare in Zimbabwe via Kenya, and then on to London. This was to attend yet another wedding, but one with a difference. A few months before I had been visited in London by my old friend, Edward Fasholé Luke II. Edward was from Sierra Leone. He had been called to the Bar in England, and now practised law in Gabarone in Botswana. He brought his fiancée, Shirley, to meet me. She was from Ghana, where her father was a judge. Edward, in his jocular way, bet me that I would not attend his wedding. My trip to Harare was to win the bet.

When I was decanted from chauffeur-driven luxury at two in the morning to check in at Bombay airport, I was lucky that the ground staff considered that I had made a mistake, as economy was packed with returning Bengali labourers. I was upgraded to first class, which was very much in conformity with everything that had happened in the last week. I arrived quite early in the morning in Nairobi with a few hours to kill, so I put my case in storage and took a taxi into town. I went to call at the office of an old friend, Philip Ransley, who practised law there. 'What are you doing here?' he asked incredulously. 'I just happened to be passing by,' I replied, 'and I thought I would take you out for lunch.' When he had got over his astonishment, he agreed, but I still had time to spare, so I went to have coffee on the terrace of the Thorn Tree Café at the New Stanley Hotel.

This is the traditional place where ex-pats meet and leave messages pinned to the trunk of the eponymous thorn tree for their friends. I was sitting alone at my table at about twelve in the morning when I was joined by two black girls, casually dressed, whom I assumed to be students. I noticed that there were plenty of empty tables, so there was no need for them to share mine. We started chatting about general subjects, until I realised that it was time for me to meet Philip. I explained that I had to go, at which point one of them offered me a threesome in a room at the hotel. I was not stupid enough for the thought that they were prostitutes not to have crossed my mind, but I had eliminated the possibility after our chat. I was surprised to be so wrong, but explained gently that I could not break my lunch date, and I doubted whether he would have approved.

The flight to Harare was uneventful, and I settled for the night into Meikle's Hotel. In those days Zimbabwe was a shining example of black/white co-operation. I had previously been involved for clients in an emerald mining deal there. I was working with the Minister of Mines, who was a Scot, and his chief civil servant, who was black, as well as the Minister for Finance, who was black, and his chief civil servant, who was white. The police did not carry guns, and it was completely safe to walk round the city at night, which I did. The only sign of shortage was the poor quality of the toilet paper. Zimbabwe was truly the jewel in the African crown. What a contrast with the present day!

The next morning, I walked to St Paul's Cathedral where the wedding was to take place. One of the prime materials in its construction was corrugated iron. It was all very different from the wedding scene that I had just left in Bombay. The service itself could best be described as 'muscular Anglican'. After monotonous Hindu chanting, the familiar hymns and psalms were almost refreshing to hear, especially sung in Edward's basso profondo voice.

I knew that, when the ceremony finished, I had to find myself a lift to the reception, which was some way away. As photographs were being taken on the Cathedral steps, I accosted an elderly, white and rather distinguished looking couple. I asked them for a lift, and they agreed. It transpired that I had picked the Chief Justice and his wife. They soon forgot the presence of their passenger, and spent the whole journey quarrelling violently as to the best way to reach their destination.

After all the lavish Indian food, traditional canapés came as something of a shock. I suddenly realised that my time was running short, and that I needed to get to the airport for my flight to London. I asked Edward for the number of a taxi service, but he informed me that he and Shirley were leaving for their honeymoon anyway, and would be delighted to take me back to the hotel to collect my case, and then on to the airport. I initially resisted, as it did not seem right to share the start of their honeymoon, but they insisted. It must have been strange for a bystander to see me decanted at departures from the front seat of a limousine bedecked with traditional wedding ribbons, and with the happy couple in the back in their full wedding finery.

13

DUBAI

Defeated by the Middle Eastern Mind Set

It was too good an offer to refuse. My friend and long-time professional collaborator, Fareed Siddiqi, a chartered accountant, had opened an office in Dubai, and wanted my firm to open a law office in parallel. He explained that you had to have a UAE fifty-one per cent partner, but in fact the local partner would be content with a nominal annual stipend for the use of his name. Clients of his there, who had helped to produce his own licence to practise, had also introduced him to an extremely well connected local lawyer there, who was prepared to help. The lawyer's uncle also happened to be the government minister responsible for issuing the necessary permits.

Fareed, Maggie and I flew out together on a Pakistan International Airways flight. Fareed had already introduced the airline to me as a client, so I was optimistic that his United Arab Emirates connections would be as good. We met our designated law partner, and I was completely bowled over. He looked like Central Casting's ideal candidate for a job as an extra in a remake of Lawrence of Arabia's *Seven Pillars of Wisdom*. Adel Habib was extremely tall and slim with a short, well-trimmed beard and a handsome face. He was dressed in spotless white robes. His English was not too good, but it was good enough for us to communicate. Although a qualified local lawyer, he had never practised. In fact, he did not need to work. His grandfather had been the surgeon to the ruling family, and Adel received a generous pension for life. He was prepared to help us for a nominal stipend, but did not expect to be called upon to work.

Fareed's man, who ran his office, was not very exciting. I realised that, if he was particularly dynamic and could bring in his own clients, you risked losing him, as he would ultimately have no need of support from the home office. Conversely, if he was not good enough to process the work that flowed into the office, there was no point in having him anyway. I knew that we would have to search hard in London for a suitable candidate to run our office, to achieve the fine balance required.

The next morning, we all had an appointment to see the Minister at eleven o'clock. We arrived in good time and were shown to seats in the corridor outside his office. Four hours later, having drunk unlimited cups of sweet, green, mint tea, we were still sitting there waiting. I now realised why I preferred dealing with Indians to Arabs. The former do not waste your time and get straight to the point. As to the latter, time seems to be meaningless.

Eventually, we were shown into the Minister's presence. His appearance did not disappoint me. Dressed in the obligatory robes, short, stout and with a hooked nose and hooded eyes, he looked as if he had come straight out of the desert. The appropriate pleasantries began, and we were served with still more cups of the wretched mint tea. After an interminable amount of time, the conversation turned to falconry, about which the Minister was passionate. My own knowledge of the subject is somewhat limited to put it mildly, and eventually I gently brought the topic of conversation round to the question of our licence to practise law in Dubai. I had obviously committed the ultimate social solecism, as we were out of the door within minutes with nothing decided, and I sensed a chill in the atmosphere.

It was all too easy for the locals. All they had to do was sit there, while the West came flocking to their door in search of business. I was told that there was one government minister whose sole job was to sit behind a desk and receive foreign businessmen, listen to their pitch, accept their brochures and other paperwork that they provided, politely dismiss them, and then throw their papers in the trash bin. All the work was done by foreigners. Europeans and Americans at the top, and vast armies of Pakistanis, Iranians and Bangladeshi labourers at the bottom. I asked why they did not empty the refugee camps, and take on the Palestinians contained within them. They could so easily have contributed to solving that problem, but it became clear that politics demanded that they left the Palestinians to rot, and looked for their cheap labour elsewhere.

Dubai was a strange mixture of a place. Unlike most of its neighbours, it did not have much oil. It had always been an *entrepôt*, and trade was essential. I was told that this had once been slavery, but more recently Dubai had grown rich on its illicit trade with India, particularly in gold and silver. In fact, it was truly a nest of smugglers and pirates. Fareed took us round to meet his clients. One of them looked as if he had stepped straight out of Long John Silver's crew in *Treasure Island*, with a change to Arab dress, but with the obligatory eye patch still in place.

You soon moved away from the picturesque creek with sleek, wooden dhows moored along the banks, to streets of newly constructed glass and concrete skyscrapers. In fact, there were many more in the course of construction with hordes of sun-darkened labourers stripped to the waist and swarming over precarious looking wooden scaffolding. To work in such extreme heat must have been almost unbearable. I was told that they lived in crowded barracks, and sent most of their wages home. Much as I loved sunbathing, I had had enough before ten in the morning, and we had not yet reached the full summer heat.

If it had not been for the encouragement of Fareed, I think I would have given up. He assured me, despite my own feelings to the contrary, that we had made a good impression and were making progress, even though I could not see it. For light relief, we drove out into the desert, but it did not thrill me. To see virtually new cars abandoned by the roadside reminded me of the story of the Arab, who, when his car ashtray became full, abandoned it, and bought another car. We also visited an indoor ice rink attached to the new and lavish Galleria Hotel complex. To see pairs of Arab men with their robes tucked up skating along and holding hands was something new and strange in my cultural experience.

We returned to London, and I reported the situation to my partners. Frankly, I would have been glad if they had said we were wasting our time, and should not continue, but they were enthusiastic, and asked me to start the search to find a suitable lawyer to run the office. I interviewed many, and eventually we chose one who had been a construction lawyer with a British company in the Gulf, and was keen to return to work there. We had two more trips out there, and I did not detect much discernible progress. I did as much fact finding as possible while there, and talked to many people. One was an English lawyer, who had married a former trainee of mine. He had been in Dubai as a partner in a large firm, and had subsequently opened up on his own. I cannot say that he was very encouraging. My chosen man kept asking me to name a starting date and, in a final effort to break the deadlock, Maggie and I, with our two small sons, booked for a Christmas holiday partly in Sharjah, the Emirate next to Dubai, and partly in Khor Fakkan, a less well known Emirate. Our motives in going were mixed. Apart from the business side, we wanted to have a good holiday in the sunshine away from the tawdry commercialism of Christmas in the West. What better place than a Muslim country?

The Holiday Inn at Khor Fakkan was fairly basic but acceptable. The beach and sea were wonderful, which kept the boys very happy. The town itself was almost non-existent, although there was a beautiful road curving along the seafront, brightly lit twenty-four hours a day with the latest sodium lights set high in gantries leading to precisely nowhere. The high spot of the week was the Costain wives' yoga class, which took place in our hotel basement. Carry-cots and pushchairs were parked at the back, while the mothers went through their exercise routines. We of course joined in. Over coffee afterwards, we realised the full extent of the plight of these poor creatures. Their husbands were engineers on contract, away all day, and they had to amuse themselves and their children in this

God-forsaken place. They talked with excitement about their weekly trip to the souk in Dubai. Having spent as few minutes as possible in the souk with its tawdry stalls selling third-rate products to second-class tourists, I envied them not at all.

Rested after a week doing virtually nothing, we moved across to the Holiday Inn at Sharjah for Christmas. We managed to hit the Gulf's annual rainstorm, and it was an odd experience to drive up the main street in our taxi, leaving a bow wave on either side, as the water was about six inches deep. Who thinks of installing drainage, when it rains so rarely?

The boys were very excited at the thought of Christmas, and it turned out that our choice was fortunate. The ruler of Sharjah allowed Christmas celebrations, while the ruler of Dubai, just down the road, did not. We sat in our room watching Bing Crosby's *White Christmas* on a tiny, black and white television, only for the film to be interrupted about every thirty minutes for the muezzin to call the faithful to prayer. I thought that Bing had the better voice.

I was tired of swimming in the hotel pool, so I decided to have a swim in the creek. It was a mistake, as I quickly found myself competing with the corpses of rotting fish, and other horrors. Despite its veneer of western sophistication, you had the feeling that the customs and conditions of the Middle Ages were just beneath the surface. Meanwhile, our now joint application for a licence to practise and a work permit for our man were getting nowhere. We had been involved now for more than nine months, and were no further forward. I have always believed in the principle of cutting my losses, and this was the time.

On returning to London, I called a partners' meeting, and we reluctantly agreed to abandon the project. Our man did not want a job in the London office, so we had to pay him off. I saw Adel Habib in London a couple of years later and he told me an interesting story. 'I must tell you about your friend, who is not your friend,' he began. The English lawyer, whom I had visited, went to see Adel, and warned him against associating with us, on the grounds that we were Jews, which was only partly true, and therefore unacceptable. I had found the attitude to Jews generally, and Israelis in particular, ambivalent in Dubai. Provided you did not parade your credentials too openly, you were free to operate. In fact, in late-night conversations the perfect trade grouping was advocated by one Arab, whose opinion I greatly respected, as consisting of Israeli technology and know-how, the massive Egyptian population, and UAE and Saudi oil. When Adel seemed unimpressed with the English lawyer's news, the latter then threatened that, if he persisted with the proposed association, he would report him to the ruler. At this Adel became angry and said that if he did, he would run him out of town, which I think he was perfectly capable of accomplishing, as he had very impressive connections. 'Anyway,' as he so nicely put it, 'Jews make the best lawyers, and I am happy to be in partnership with the best.'

Sadly, Adel did not prosper. The life of leisure and unlimited money did him no good. I heard years later that he died of a heroin overdose.

Our failure to get our permits turned out to be a blessing in disguise. Within months of our last trip, the whole Gulf economy was blown away by a catastrophic drop in the price of oil. Construction projects ceased overnight, and the overseas workforce was sent packing, often without payment. The Europeans and Americans left in a hurry and the whole place reverted for the time being to a small, desert port. Fareed had to close his office and pay off his man. Our losses, if we had continued, would have been much greater than the small amount we had expended, which we put down to experience anyway.

14

MR SHAHANI

My Super Hospitable Voyeur

Mr Shahani, yet another Indian business client, was my fairytale prince. He had been an unimportant client of the firm before I joined in 1961. While he operated a worldwide empire of small, largely retail, businesses, London was only the financing and communications hub. Apart from the odd lease renewal, or piece of minor litigation, there was nothing more to expect from him. Yet he seemed to take a shine to me. With homes all over the world, and his wife and four children not spending too much time in London, he would breeze into town and invite me out to lunch. I think many people had difficulty understanding his machine-gun-like delivery, but I could manage it.

Sometimes lunch was at the London International Rotary Club at the Café Royal in Regent Street, but more often it was a visit to the Playboy Club in Park Lane, which I realised Mr Shahani considered as the height of vice. The bunny girls' uniforms were so much from a past age. Their compressed cleavages were anything but an aphrodisiac, and it always amused me how their un-tanned patches of white, where their bikini bottoms covered them, showed through their semi-sheer stockings. It was a matter of look, titillate, but never touch.

Mr Shahani liked to talk about his various businesses, and I came up with the idea of grouping his various entities with a possible view to a public flotation, and certainly with succession planning in mind. His oldest sons were already in the business, and he was very proud that the youngest was going to Eton, the first of his community to take that step. He expressed enthusiasm for my ideas, and asked me to make a trip to Gibraltar, where he had a number of shops. With the benefit of hindsight, I think he was humouring me on my ideas. He was lonely, and just wanted company. He was the most polite man that I have ever met. If I sneezed, he too would sneeze to make me feel good.

I duly flew out to Gibraltar. It is the first and only time that I have walked from the terminal into town with my suitcase. The Shahani principal shop on Main Street was easy to find, and I was given a tour of his other businesses and the whole Rock. It did not take too long. Pictures of British royalty were everywhere. The population was mixed, although predominantly Spanish. I found this loyalty to the Crown a little touching, though I feared that it was largely based on self-interest. British government subsidies made life very easy, and they would not be replaced if the Rock became just another part of Spain.

I was put up at the Queens Hotel, and the high spot of the day for Mr Shahani was our lunch with the Prime Minister of the Rock, Sir Joshua Hassan, who also doubled as his lawyer. The concept of conflict of interest troubled nobody. Sir Joshua always ate caviar followed by fillet steak, washed down with a vintage claret, so Mr Shahani was careful to see that the kitchen had plenty of all three. It was an extremely pleasant lunch designed to put me at my ease. With a host like that, there was no problem.

The next day, we set out on the ferry to Algeciras. Spain at the time had closed the land borders with Gibraltar to all except domestic servants and other lower-paid workers. We hired a car and Mr Shahani drove me slowly along the Spanish coast as far as Torremolinos and Marbella. We detoured to the Spanish side of the border with Gibraltar at La Linea, so that I could see the magnificent house, which he had had built, but left empty. We had a great lunch at the Club in Marbella, and spent the evening touring the slightly risqué bars of Torremolinos, where scantily clad mainly Swedish girls were draped in the softly lit windows as an invitation to enter. It reminded me of James Michener's *The Drifters*. As an example of vice, it was rather tame, but I was coming to the view that Mr Shahani got a kick out of leading me on, even though I was scarcely thrilled.

All pretence of talking about work was long gone, and we were definitely on holiday. The next day, we retraced our steps to Algeciras, and took another ferry to Tangier in Morocco. When we arrived, immigration formalities were a pain, as we had to line up for a couple of hours in the noonday heat, but I very much enjoyed my first visit to Tangier. We had a magnificent lunch, which was couscous based, and after touring the palaces and souks, we caught the last ferry back to Gibraltar. The next day, laden down with curios gifted from his shops, I said goodbye to Mr Shahani and flew back to London. I did produce a feasibility study on the proposed project, but it would not surprise me if Mr Shahani never read it.

The next trip followed a few months later. This time we flew together to Tenerife, where Mr Shahani owned a commercial hotel, as well as the usual duty free shops, catering particularly to the passengers from the cruise ships. We toured the island exhaustively by car, and once again it was easy to forget the supposed purpose of my visit. That evening at dinner, Mr Shahani announced out of the blue that we were going to a brothel. I narrowly avoided choking on my soup. Santa Cruz de Tenerife is a thriving port as well as the commercial capital of the island. I did not know what to expect. We took a taxi through increasingly characterless outer suburbs with the usual semi-detached houses. It could have been Wembley, where I was born. Eventually, we reached a street corner, and Mr Shahani sent the taxi driver to find out what was happening at the supposed brothel.

It was about nine-fifteen p.m., and when a wooden window opened in the nondescript door, words in Spanish were exchanged. The driver came back to the car to announce that the brothel was already closed for the evening. So much for Santa Cruz nightlife, and I breathed a sigh of relief, which turned out to be premature. Mr Shahani had already made it his night's ambition to get me laid.

We drove to a shabby, shanty-like building in the port area with some sort of neon lighting outside. Inside, the lights were very low, and on my patron's urging, I asked one of the ladies at the bar to dance. She was extremely well upholstered, and, after the large amount I had already drunk that evening, it was quite pleasant to rest my weary limbs on her, while we shuffled round the floor to smash hits of the forties and fifties in the company of various nondescript sailors and their girls.

All good things must come to an end. The music stopped and bright fluorescent lighting was suddenly switched on. I received a terrible shock to realise that I had not so much been dancing with someone of my mother's age, but more like my grandmother's. She now went into her commercial pitch. Her English was fairly inadequate for most purposes, but clearly she had had practice with this one. 'You like ze spank?' she asked. At first I did not understand, and asked her to repeat the question, which she did. 'All Englishmen like ze spank.' I corrected her by saying that this particular Englishman had no desire to give or receive corporal punishment, or anything else for that matter from somebody who was a contemporary of his grandmother.

I think Mr Shahani was disappointed, as I saw that he already had his wallet out, and was fishing in it for the price of the proposed add-on services. We spent one more night in Tenerife. Mr Shahani announced that we were going to his club to play gin rummy. I took one look around and decided that I needed a walk and some fresh air. I left him and his friends to it, and soon noticed, opposite, a lively disco, where the average age was about fifteen. Nobody took the slightest notice of me, and I vigorously danced away my surplus energy. When I went back, I assured them that I had enjoyed my walk.

The next day, we flew to Madrid and stayed at the Ritz, which was old fashioned, but magnificent. I had a superb suite completely to myself. That evening, after another great dinner, we gravitated to the sleazy but up-market end of the city. We entered a basement club, which promised much in the way of sexual delights, but delivered little. The two of us were taken in hand, literally as well as metaphorically, by a lively and pretty girl from deepest Surrey. She was being paid a commission for each drink we consumed, and I was open mouthed with admiration at the efficient way she went about her job. She deserved the Queen's Award for Industry. I was even more admiring when I realised that she had another group of punters at the other end of the bar, whom she was similarly plying. She would make an excuse to leave us for a few minutes to service the other group, and then vice versa.

I was beginning to flag from the late nights, and Mr Shahani saw me yawning, so characteristically offered me the chance, which I took, to cut the evening short. The next day I flew back to London, and sadly that was the end of our trips together. I clearly disappointed him. If I had been willing to play the great sexual ram, they would probably have continued. People get their kicks in many different ways, and he was obviously something of a charming voyeur. He has been dead a number of years now, but I would not put it past him to sniff out some sleazy cabaret in St Peter's domain and take his celestial lawyer along for a risqué ride.

15

ZAMBIA, ZIMBABWE, KENYA

An African Whirlwind

I thought that my fascination with Africa would gradually die out, but I was wrong. I constantly had mental pictures of elephants scratching their backsides on trees, to the point that the trees were uprooted, the soil was blown away and new desert was created. It was sheer ignorance to oppose the culling of elephants. Then again, driving in the country behind a diesel lorry, which lacked any maintenance and was therefore spewing foul, black exhaust smoke into the trees did not make me despair, but on the contrary made me want to do something about the problem. It was a pleasure to act for Prince Sadruddin's charity based in Geneva, the object of which was to provide stoves in African villages, which slow burnt minimal wood so that the villagers need not continue to cut down trees indiscriminately, with the result that deforestation was considerably slowed.

My own firm was expanding at such a rate that I realised I needed to learn more about the art or science of management – all these years later, I still do not know which it is – in order to run the practice efficiently. Perhaps typically, I went overboard in my search for knowledge, and came back, especially from America, with impractical ideas which frightened my partners. As a result, I became frustrated, and developed a parallel practice as a management consultant specialising in the professional practice area, but in lawyers in particular. I was writing articles and lecturing on the subject, and I was pleased when the then deputy editor of *The Law*

Society Gazette asked me to put together a series of articles, which I had written for it, in book form. *Anatomy of Professional Practice* sold quite well within the profession, but to me the exposure was more important than the cash.

Its successor, *Successful Mergers*, was a much better book. I acted as general editor, and wrote those chapters where I could not find a better author. Unfortunately, it was published by Waterlows, part of the Robert Maxwell empire. The book was launched with a great party, but then sank, to continue the watery metaphor, when Maxwell himself drowned. Any royalties earned were enjoyed by the company's administrators.

I had become very much involved in the International Bar Association (IBA) and particularly its Practice Management and Technology Committee, which I ultimately chaired for four very satisfying years. I found many kindred spirits in the IBA, who wanted to bring advanced ideas of law and practice to the developing world. I was able to sell my proposal for a one-man lecture tour to Zambia, Zimbabwe and Kenya relatively easily. The subject matter was practice management and allied issues. I was prepared to donate my professional time, and the IBA Educational Trust and the Commonwealth Lawyers Association shared the expenses jointly.

I flew out to Lusaka in Zambia, and received a red carpet welcome. I was met literally off the plane, and whisked through Immigration and Customs. The hotel was something of an anti-climax, more like a prison. I was emphatically warned that I must not go out alone. I did not find it too unpleasant to be marooned by the poolside in the day after the rigours of the English winter. My hosts took me out for a great dinner, which was somewhat spoilt, at least for them, by the discovery afterwards that all the hubcaps were missing from their car. I privately resolved not to challenge the ban on leaving the hotel on my own any further.

The next day was billed as a six-hour solo performance by me, and I have to say that I was delighted when the Attorney General hogged the microphone for nearly two hours of that time. The following day, I did a half-day seminar on the new British Immigration and Nationality Law, so I was keeping fairly busy. I had been warned that President Kaunda, having by then been in office for many years, had become characteristically paranoid. I was therefore not pleased to receive a number of telephone calls from Humphrey Malemba, who was in town. Humphrey had been the unsuccessful presidential candidate against Kaunda at the last election. His punishment was to be appointed Zambian High Commissioner in Ottawa, far enough away not to be a threat. He had consulted me on some matters in London, so he had a perfectly good reason to approach me in Lusaka, but I was nevertheless worried.

That worry turned out to be well justified, when I went up to my room to find the door, which I had left locked, half open, with all my belongings in disarray, although nothing was missing. That evening, I was having dinner with an Indian industrialist, who was a client in London, in the Holiday Inn. He suddenly leaned across the table and told me to keep my voice down. 'Those two men at the next table are listening to every word you say – they are security agents.' I replied, 'How do we know they are not listening to you?' 'Believe me,' he whispered, 'you are the one who interests them.' When I left from Lusaka Airport, it was with a profound sense of relief. I had already written in my mind some very disturbing newspaper headlines about my detention without trial. I realised that I am not of the stuff from which martyrs are made.

My welcome at Harare Airport was more low key, but still extremely pleasant. Neil Ralston, the president of the Zimbabwe Law Society, was outside the arrivals gate and drove me to the comfort of Meikles Hotel. The next day was billed as another six-hour solo effort, but this time there was no respite. I was asked if I minded the performance being videoed, so that it could be shown in Bulawayo as well. At first, I was a little self-conscious in front of the camera, but I soon forgot about it. At one stage in the day, I came out with the immortal words 'here in Zambia'. Neil, who was chairing the session, corrected me sotto voce, 'Zimbabwe'. I immediately understood President Reagan's well-known propensity to make gaffes of this nature. It was not caused by stupidity, but by perfectly understandable confusion due to fatigue and the pace of modern travel.

Neil asked me what I wanted to do that evening. I think I shocked him when I told him that I wanted to go back to the hotel and, Garbo-like, be alone. The thought of any more personal projection or communication was complete anathema to me. I went down to the dining room and found a table near the band, an excellent South African group, which played my requests for the rest of the evening. The first bottle of wine that I ordered was a local one called Gue. After one glass, I sent it back as it tasted horrible, and I altered the wine list with my pen to identify it as 'Glue'. The next bottle was labelled South African and much better. It had a Latin sounding name. I then remembered that I had drunk the same wine in Zambia, where the waiter described it as Portuguese. As any mention of South Africa in Zambia was always coupled with the epithets 'fascist, imperialistic, colonialist', it was not hard to understand why the origin was concealed. Hypocrisy was well and truly alive in our former colonies.

The next day, I lectured Neil's firm on strategic planning and other subjects. It was a pleasure to see an obviously harmonious mix of blacks and whites, though Neil confided to me that they had trouble holding on to the black lawyers, once they qualified, as they could make so much more money by taking up any number of well paid posts as non-executive directors, which were virtually sinecures. That evening the Law Society secretary, Barry Brighton, gave me the choice of dinner in a restaurant, or at his house. I jumped at the idea of home cooking after wall-to-wall restaurants. Barry and his wife, Sue, gave me a marvellous evening.

I flew off to Nairobi the next day to meet Maggie, who was coming out from London, so that we could have a few days holiday in conjunction with my lecturing. I have already talked about my welcomes at Lusaka and Harare airports. Here there was none. We checked into the New Stanley Hotel, and the next day I phoned the Law Society, who denied any knowledge of either my mission or me. Deciding that we would extend the holiday element, I was on the phone to the concierge to find us a hotel near Mombasa for the weekend. While idly leafing through the *Nation* – the local paper – at the same time, I nearly dropped the phone when I noticed quite a small advertisement for my talk, which was scheduled for the next afternoon. They nearly lost me.

The day after my talk, we joined up with a group of English lawyers, who travelled the world under the banner, 'Tax in the Sun'. Meticulously run by Richard Rawlence and Anthony Slingsby, their first trip many years before was for a long weekend to a skyscraper hotel at La Manga on one of the Costas in Spain. Both the electricity and the water there failed. As Maggie and I were on the seventeenth floor, this was a bit of a hardship as obviously the lifts were not working. I thought that I was being very ingenious to use the melted ice in the silver bucket, containing the ubiquitous welcome bottle of Spanish champagne, for shaving purposes, only to find that every other man had done the same thing. A day's tax lectures followed, so it could be said that the object of the excursion was not sheer pleasure.

Those trips evolved into an annual event, and we became more and more adventurous in the choice of destinations. The classic, showing our leaders' versatility, was a proposed golfing trip to Marbella, carrying a silver cup for the tournament winner, which had to abort at the eleventh hour in the face of a total strike by Spanish Air Traffic Control personnel. After a round of frantic telephone calls at the South Mimms Motel, where we had gathered on the way to Luton Airport, we were offered as an alternative an immediate trip to Istanbul on Turkish Airlines. This was not such a great offer as it sounded, as a Boeing of Turkish Airlines had gone down near Paris shortly before with the loss of all on board. The faint-hearted slunk off, but the rest of us went for it. I was amused by the division between smoking and non-smoking passengers on Turkish Airlines. Smoking passengers sat to port, and non-smoking to starboard. It was all rather like *Alice in Wonderland*.

We had a great time, especially when wandering round the city's bazaars trying to exchange pocketfuls of Spanish pesetas for local goods. As there was no local golf course available, the cup was awarded for the best poem written on the trip. My years of composing Latin hexameters and Greek iambics were not wasted, and I won the cup. In fact, in future years the cup was always given for poetry, and I was eventually barred from competing as I was too successful. Over the years, a great camaraderie grew between us, and I was extremely pleased when it was announced that our trip coincided with their safari tour, and that I had been invited to lecture them.

We met up in Nairobi and had a couple of superb days on safari. Things had changed much for the better since our own amateur attempts in Tsavo Game Reserve a number of years before. Nowadays, it was more like a theatrical performance, as we sat in our comfortable armchairs sipping good wine, while the animals, oblivious to our presence, because of the position of the floodlights and the plate glass between us, came down to the watering hole. We also opted for the somewhat less comfortable option of being woken by buzzer through the night, when something interesting happened on stage. Wrapped in blankets, we watched all sorts of wild animals fighting, mating, eating, drinking, licking salt, and otherwise behaving naturally. I saw that the buffalo, rather than the lion, is the true king of the jungle.

The next day, I gave my lecture under tropical trees and surrounded by beautiful flowers. We had to leave the group and return to Nairobi. By now, I had clocked up twenty-three hours lecturing. I was asked by a local lawyer to be his guest at a Rotary Club lunch. When we arrived, we were told that the speaker had cancelled at the last moment. You can guess who stepped into the breach. I talked about the new British dynamic under Margaret Thatcher and clocked up my full twenty-four hours of speaking on the tour.

16

IRFAN OSMAN

Loneliness, Generosity and Ultimate Sadness

Irfan Osman was my perfect client. He left me to get on with the job, and never complained if the outcome was not as he had expected. He was born in the Turkish section of Cyprus, where he had been a magistrate. He came to London and read for the Bar. I first met him when I was an articled clerk instructing Hiram Powell, a barrister, for whom Irfan was a pupil. We kept in touch, and he became a client when I joined Anthony Sumption. He did not practise as a barrister, but worked for one of the large insurance brokerages, and was involved in their inheritance tax saving schemes. He then formed his own company in the wealth management field. Clearly he was prospering, but I somehow felt that I did not want to know in detail how he made his money. In the climate of the times, I had no problems with tax avoidance, but did not wish to be involved with tax evasion, or that halfway house, 'avoision'.

As a client, Irfan felt that he should do more for his professional advisers, and I was happy to be a beneficiary of his munificence. He told me that he was in control of a large cabin cruiser, *Seadrift*, which was owned by construction clients of his in the North of England. The boat was then moored at Antibes in France, and as nobody was using it in late October to early November, would I like to have a free family holiday for two weeks? Of course I accepted, especially when he told me that the boat was run by a husband and wife team, and that she was a cordon-bleu chef.

We duly flew out to Nice and joined the boat at Antibes marina. Our party consisted of Maggie, our two boys, the current au pair and me. There was plenty of room on board, and we duly set sail along the Mediterranean coast in an easterly direction. We anchored in the beautiful bay of Villefranche, and, after using the hand-pumped lavatory, I decided to go down the ladder for a swim. I was enjoying myself greatly, until I realised that I was fast approaching an area copiously dotted with my own excrement. I had a lot to learn about life at sea.

That evening we moored at one of the Nice marinas. At this time of the year, there was no need to book in advance, and there was always a berth for us. As Mary's cooking was so good, we arranged to stay two nights each time we stopped. On one evening we would eat on board, while we would sample the local restaurants on the other. One problem with a holiday at that time of the year was the uncertain weather. That evening, there was a torrential rainstorm. Walking down what to me seemed a very flimsy gangway, my feet slipped, and I found myself by some contortion under the gangway, holding on desperately. As I was face down, I was able to see the filthy condition of the water, and that alone was sufficient encouragement for me to make an almost superhuman effort, and pull myself up to safety.

The visitors' book in the main cabin gave me the clue as to the normal use of the boat. It clearly existed to provide holidays for North Country councillors and their officials. Irfan had already told me that the boat's owners were big in local authority construction projects, so it was easy for me to put two and two together, to make six. After some thought, I saw no reason for this to spoil our holiday. We slowly meandered along the coast like luxurious, water-borne gypsies. Monte Carlo proved something of a diversion. After eating dinner at the rooftop restaurant of the Hotel de Paris with its incredible opening roof, and an hour spent at the casino watching particularly the extreme concentration on the faces of the gamblers, which a bomb loudly exploding in the square outside was unlikely to disturb, we were taken out to drinks at their apartment by elderly clients. We waited on the steps of the casino, until a vintage Rolls-Royce chugged into view. We then slowly drove about two hundred yards around the square to their apartment block. It would have been much quicker to walk. It was no surprise that the car had recorded less than ten thousand miles in its whole venerable existence.

We continued as far as San Remo in Italy. The contrast between its rather tatty and run-down casino and the magnificence of that of Monte Carlo was marked. We then retraced our steps, equally slowly, to Antibes, and said our fond farewells to David and Mary, who had looked after us so well. Edward, our three-year-old son, after ten minutes with David at the wheel, was convinced that he was an accomplished sailor.

Irfan offered us *Seadrift* again the following year in the spring. This time the boat was moored at Piraeus, so we flew to Athens. The construction industry in Britain had suffered a downturn, so I understood the problem when a worried David told me that we could not leave port because of the problem of unpaid harbour dues. This gave us the chance to explore Athens, both ancient and modern, in detail, although it did nothing for our lungs, as you could actually see the exhaust pollution hanging in the air.

The outstanding debt was magically paid, and we were off on a tour of the Greek Islands, which were almost free of tourists at that time of the year. Despite the obvious lack of water, the wild spring flowers were a delight. Aegina was a little disappointing, but Poros was very interesting, with its naval base, and particularly an ancient Monitor from the First World War, which was moored with its huge gun facing out to sea and threatening nobody in particular. The only other boats that we saw were the ubiquitous Blue Dolphins, which formed the regular transport around the islands. They always seemed filled with passengers, but strangely we hardly saw any people on land.

Our favourite island was Hydra. It must have been hell on earth at the height of the tourist season in mid-summer, but now we had the place to ourselves. We tended to stick to Mary's cooking, as I have an aversion to the lukewarm food that the Greeks almost invariably provided. Thank heaven they have learned their lesson, and Greek food in London and New York is heated to the right temperature. One of our delights was to sit on the quay, drinking our morning coffee, and watching the water supply boat dock with its deck almost level with the sea, then to see it depart empty a few hours later, after its contents were pumped out, sitting immensely high in the water.

We went on to the mainland at Naphlion, and climbed the very many steps to the medieval castle at the top. This was as far as we could go, before our return to the bustle of Piraeus. There were no more invitations to spend time on *Seadrift*. Perhaps the supply of nautically-minded local authority councillors and employees had come to an end. I doubt if they paid any more for their pleasure than we did.

After the demise of *Seadrift*, Irfan's bounty had not come to an end. He had bought a flat in Cannes and wanted us to have a holiday there. In addition, he provided us with our flights free, and announced that not only was a BMW waiting for us in the garage of the block, but that an amount of spending money was ready for us to collect on presenting ourselves to his bank in Cannes.

The flat was in a newly-built block just off the Croisette on a main one-way road, where the lorries needed to change gear on their way out of the town. Every evening, along the blank wall opposite, the local prostitutes gathered to ply their trade, but with the windows shut and the curtains drawn, the ambience was delightful. We disgraced ourselves by spending the not inconsiderable sum of money available to us on a magnificent meal at the Palme d'Or. It was a case of easy come, easy go. The car turned out to be almost a wasted luxury. Being used to driving all the time in London, it was a pleasure to walk around Cannes, which is so much more compact, especially as we knew the surrounding countryside fairly well from previous trips.

Our annual visits to Cannes as guests of Irfan continued for a number of years, even though the additional perks were gradually withdrawn. His home life was not a happy one. His wife was a difficult woman, and they virtually lived apart. He was only able to keep her quiet with frequent gifts of large sums of money. His son, Gordon, sadly was autistic. This did not suppress his sex drive, and Gordon roamed the world on an American Express card supplied by his father, getting into all sorts of trouble. On one occasion, after a visit to Israel, he arrived back at Heathrow with a potential bride. In her interview, the immigration officer was so disparaging of Gordon as a future husband that the bride-to-be turned around and went home.

On his return from a business trip to Panama (I did not enquire as to the nature of the business), Irfan swore that he had been poisoned. He had already told me that his philosophy was to die without leaving any assets or liabilities. He now went into a steady decline. As he lived quite near me, in a large mansion on his own, I used to go over and do what I could for him, but, as the end approached, his wife suddenly swooped, and took him away.

He had acquired residence rights in Switzerland, and built a beautiful house there. I had seen his Swiss Will, where he asked to be buried on a hillside overlooking the Alps, and for a marble mausoleum to be erected over his grave. Close family apart, his bank manager from Coutts and I were the only people at the bleak cemetery on a windswept hillside outside Bath. His wife, whom I knew had personally received millions, especially in the last few years, gave him the cheapest Co-op funeral possible. She had even refused a limousine to accompany the hearse, in order to save a few pounds. There was no minister present, and nobody said a word. Gordon came up to me and said sadly, 'I don't have a daddy any more.' The family left in their cars in great haste with hardly a word of farewell, still less of apology.

The bank manager and I were effectively marooned without transport some miles from the city. Fortunately, the funeral team from the Co-op took pity on us, and gave us a lift to the station in the hearse. Irfan proved just how difficult it is to die with a nil estate. He seriously miscalculated, and left a number of debts, which included a substantial one to my firm for outstanding legal fees. I could hardly complain.

17

JERSEY

Shady Business Degenerating into Farce

I was fascinated by Syd Lipman. We were only about five years apart in age, but in truth he came from my father's generation. Brought up in the East End of London, he must have been exceptionally gifted to get as far as he did as a chartered accountant. He was a compulsive womaniser, and I felt that, deep down, he must hate the whole sex to behave as he did. When I eventually met his wife, she was extremely cold to me. I asked Syd for an explanation, and he told me that he used my name very often as a cover for his nocturnal escapades, to the point that she thought I was leading him astray.

The showdown came when Syd came to see me, more angry than distressed, to announce that he was divorcing his wife. He had been entertaining one of his women in a room in the White House, a hotel in London once famous for such activities, and on coming down in the lift after his assignation had met his wife waiting to enter it, hand in hand with the family dentist. Their intentions were obviously the same as his had been. I fell about laughing, but he could not see the funny side. 'But the *dentist*,' he kept repeating. I could not persuade him that there was rough justice in the situation – what's sauce for the goose is sauce for the gander, or vice versa.

He did divorce her, but I refused to act for him. Characteristically, though, he then installed his ex-wife as his mistress. Syd was an extremely orthodox Jew, and he could not see that his sexual behaviour was in complete contradiction to his other life. He then met and fell in love with Margaret, a Christian lady, who worked in his office building. He would only marry her if she converted to Judaism. As his was a particularly orthodox sect, she had to be billeted with a strictly religious family in North London and taught the intricacies of the religion. Her motive in converting had to be her attraction to Judaism, and not her attraction to Syd. Unfortunately, an ill-wisher denounced them to the Beth Din, the rabbinical court which governs such matters, and they both had to go before a trio of rabbis and swear that they hardly knew each other, and certainly had no plans to marry.

Like so many converts, Margaret, now renamed Sarah, took to the religion like a duck to water, and became more extreme than Syd. Maggie and I were invited round for dinner to their home, and I noticed a rather fine portrait of a bearded old man on the wall. I assumed it was Syd's grandfather, but it turned out to be some rabbi in New York, who governed every step of Sarah's new life.

Continuing his double life, one holiday Syd installed Sarah, her granddaughter, Rebecca, on whom he doted as a loving step-grandfather, and the au pair in a flat, which he owned, in Tel Aviv, while he took a suite down the road in the Hilton, which he shared with Marion, his ex-wife and current mistress. He used the excuse that he needed rest after working so hard, and the presence of Rebecca distracted him.

What I also found extraordinary about Syd was his ability to mix with ease in all levels of society, despite the limitations of his own upbringing. We shared a number of clients, and I had difficulty connecting with the East End and Essex fraternity. They found me a bit too posh; though my own origins were hardly superior. So much for the benefits of education. I learned a lot from Syd. When a group of us went to hear jazz at Ronnie Scott's, Ronnie Scott himself and Syd were lost to the rest of us for half an hour, as it transpired that they were in the same class at school and needed to catch up. I learned that the boxing promoter, Micky Duff, was originally Moishe Deutsch, and that the singer, Georgia Brown, was born Lily Klot. I queried the latter piece of information, only to find it confirmed by her obituary in *The Times*. Taking a taxi ride with Syd was usually a treat, as half London's taxi drivers seemed to have been at school with him, and we rarely paid for our ride, and certainly never needed to tip.

When Leslie Carey, a mutual client, who ran a chain of betting shops in East London and Essex, asked us to join him on a visit to Jersey, to buy a betting shop chain there, I was looking forward to the trip. Until the government of the day changed the law, Leslie operated as an illegal bookmaker from his back parlour in Romford, Essex. When betting shops were suddenly legalised, Leslie acquired a lot of them, and became extremely rich. He was one of the clients to whom I had difficulty relating. Both Syd and I felt we were in professional difficulty when Leslie announced that he was proposing to carry the cash for the purchase with him on the flight to Jersey. This was contrary to the Exchange Control Law, which then applied. I persuaded Syd that we should fly out on a different plane, to distance ourselves from a potentially perilous situation.

We left Heathrow on a small plane, and I found to my surprise that Syd was a very nervous flyer. When we touched down at Jersey airport, the plane lurched sideways, and we taxied to a far corner of the airfield, with one of the wheels going 'bump, bump, bump, bump', as fire engines and ambulances with sirens screaming hurtled towards us, seemingly from all directions. 'What's happening?' asked Syd, in a voice of terror. 'I suppose it's a burst tyre,' I replied almost nonchalantly. I was right. When we disembarked, the plane had a substantial sideways list, and a shredded tyre.

Leslie was waiting for us clutching an enormous paper carrier bag, which he told us contained the money. We went in a taxi to the house of Mr Cohen, the owner of the business, where the details of the deal were to be worked out. Three hours later, we were still negotiating, and needed to adjourn for lunch. We were sitting down at a table at a local restaurant, when Leslie shot into the air as though stung by a bee. 'The money!' he shouted. He had left the carrier bag in the middle of Mr Cohen's living room. He dashed out, and returned triumphantly a short time later, clutching the bag to his ample midriff.

We resumed negotiations, but clearly no deal was to be reached that day, and we had to catch the last flight home. None of us were enamoured by the prospect of spending the night in Jersey. But what were we to do with the money? It was tempting providence to take it on a flight again, so we had to find a bank prepared to accept it. We trudged up and down the main street of St Helier meeting refusal after refusal. No bank wanted our money, even thought we were prepared to pay them interest for the privilege of holding it. Eventually, we found one which would, and we then had to endure the lengthy process while a veritable array of bank staff counted and re-counted it.

Finally, Syd and I boarded our small plane. Syd was again in a very nervous state. I ventured to reassure him. 'Never mind, lightning never strikes twice in the same place.' I was wrong. We hit the mother and father of electrical storms as we neared Heathrow. The plane bucked and lurched as we endlessly circled the airport. 'Hold my hand, hold my hand!' implored Syd. I could do nothing else, and he responded by digging his fingernails in panic into my flesh, to the point that I was left with deep indentations for days. Just as we were cleared for landing, Syd vomited tidily into the receptacle provided. I never flew with him again.

His life did not end well. Sarah and I were appointed his executors, and I devised a Will, which was designed to strike a balance between his first and second families. Syd assumed that, as his father had lived well into his nineties, he was destined to do the same. I was shocked one day, when I phoned him to arrange one of our regular dinners in the greasy kosher restaurant which he insisted on frequenting, by his uncharacteristically gloomy tone. His doctor had told him that he had cancer of the pancreas, and that he had six weeks to live. I insisted that we have our dinner, but the doctor was right, and he lasted a precise six weeks.

All hell now broke loose. Sarah, his widow and my co-executor, insisted that millions in cash was missing from the house. She accused her stepdaughter, who fortunately was able to exonerate herself. She then accused my partner, who was dealing with the probate, and by implication me, of stealing the money, though we had never been near the house. She then refused to co-operate in the administration of the estate and instructed other lawyers to bring an action claiming a larger share of the estate than Syd had wanted to give her. I pointed out gently that she was technically suing herself as an executor, but she would not listen.

I was greatly helped and comforted during this time by Barry Lewis, Syd's former partner in the accounting practice, from whom he had become estranged. I now learned from Barry that Sarah had been the reason. We were at a complete impasse, until one day on returning to the office and listening to my voicemail messages, I heard Barry's voice cheerfully singing Harold Arlen's well known song from *The Wizard of Oz*, 'Ding dong, the wicked witch, the wicked witch, ding dong the wicked witch is dead.'

Sarah, whom Syd had been convinced was destined to pre-decease him, had at last died, and made things easy for us. On the face of it, Syd and I had very little in common but I miss him to this day.

18

VANCOUVER

Take the Money and Fly

I was becoming more and more involved in the overseas conference scene. I understood how Commander Whitehead and David
Ogilvy had carried all before them in the USA. My English accent
completely compensated for any deficiencies in content or delivery.
On one occasion I was actually ambushed by a group of 'fans.' 'Say
something to us. It doesn't matter what. We just love your British
accent.' The truth was that I was running away from the problems
at home. It had always been my ambition to build up a substantial
law firm from the time that I joined Anthony Sumption in 1961,
when we were two partners with a staff of three. By 1985, I was the
senior of twenty partners with a staff approaching a hundred and
fifty in number. To the outside world I was an utter success, but I
felt that I had built myself a prison. I disliked most of my partners,
and felt that they did not share my aspirations and ambitions. They
were all for safety first and the status quo, worshipping the quantity
of work rather than the quality. I was still ambitious. The fault
had to be largely mine. I had been in too much of a hurry, and
surrounded myself with the wrong people. I had also failed to
communicate my vision, and enthuse those around me.

I could justify these overseas trips in marketing terms, as I rarely
failed to come back with, if not actual work, at least contacts to law
firms, which would give us business, when they had it. I was also
improving my management skills by exposure to the best minds in that
field in the USA. Without attending Harvard Business School, I was

getting the benefit, and I was finding much more stimulation from these new endeavours than I now obtained from the practice of law.

I attended a five-day course on strategic planning at Michigan Law School in Ann Arbor, and made sufficient of a nuisance of myself to be invited to join the faculty for the next seminar of the Institute of Continuing Legal Education that summer in San Francisco. This was a great improvement on February in Ann Arbor, where I had never been so cold in my life. At the San Francisco seminar, I acquired as a client a large mid-western law firm, which sent me for years a continuing stream of substantial and interesting work, which more than justified the cost of trip. On the last day, I was buttonholed by a delegate who asked me if I would be the guest speaker at the annual dinner of the Vancouver chapter of the Association of Legal Administrators. This type of on the spot invitation is very common, but only very rarely materialises into a concrete opportunity.

This one was the exception, and I duly received a written invitation, asking me to name my terms. I had already been to Vancouver on business, and I had not enjoyed it. I found the people stuffy and unfriendly. It also always seemed to rain. Any government which insisted on printing all public notices in English and French, where nobody spoke French, was stupid and not for me. My case in Vancouver was ongoing, and needed a personal push, but I was very busy in London, so I put forward what I considered an unacceptable and outrageous package. In addition to a fee of £1,000, I asked for first-class air travel, two nights at the Four Seasons, and all other expenses. When the acceptance came by return, I was dumbfounded, and had to say yes.

I needed as much time as possible in the office. Therefore, instead of flying direct to Vancouver on an earlier flight, I booked a later flight on British Airways to Seattle, with an onward connection to Vancouver, which was due to arrive in time for me to check into my hotel, and be ready for the evening. My hosts had omitted to give me the starting time. The flight to Seattle was a non-stop party. There were a number of British Airways' captains on board who were going to Boeing for training, and to pick up new planes. I sobered up quickly when the pilot announced over the tannoy that we were having to circle Seattle, as there was a surge of arriving flights due to the fact that Vancouver airport was closed because of snow. I had visions of having to set up a video link in Seattle and deliver my speech by long distance.

I sprinted off the plane to the connection desk, and managed to talk my way on to the first flight out to Vancouver, which had started checking in at that moment. I was sitting on the flight next to a very charming Canadian bank manager. I asked her when events of this type usually began, and she reassured me by saying that eight p.m. was the norm. She kindly gave me a lift into town, and I saw that Vancouver is like London, in that an inch of snow completely paralyses the city.

I was just settling into my room at the Four Seasons, when the phone rang. 'Where are you?' was the question. 'We're downstairs, and waiting to take you to the venue. Cocktails start in thirty minutes.' I hastily tried to repair the ravages caused by too much champagne, a ten-hour flight and eight hours time difference. The walk to the meeting was miserable, as the snow came over the top of my Gucci-style loafers. I had not thought to pack anything more substantial, as it never snows in Vancouver, or so I thought.

I delivered my speech on autopilot, and managed to answer coherently those questions that followed, but I was seriously flagging. I realised it was all too much when I was asked to join the group in the bar after dinner. Sleep was more important. The next day I felt terrible, but managed to brief the local lawyers to get our case moving. The client had been delighted when I had told him that I was going back to Vancouver, and that he need not contribute to the expense of the trip.

Was it worth it? I am not sure that my audience got full value for their money. You obviously have to pay big bucks to attract outside speakers to a remote place like Vancouver. For my part, I had to deal with severe jet lag for a week, which inhibited my performance, but overall it was fun, and something different.

19

NIGERIA

What Lies Beneath the Welcome Smile

PART 1

Nigeria was one country that I had no ambition to visit. I seemed to have been adopted by the Sindhi community of Indians. They were mostly Hindus, though the notable exception was the Bhutto family, which was Muslim, and provided two presidents for Pakistan, both of whom met a tragic end. On the partition of India, the Sindhis in effect became a displaced people, as Sindh was made part of Pakistan. They were compelled to use their talents in business in places where others were reluctant to go. I learned to cast an expert eye over duty-free shops. So often they were Sindhi owned, and formed the basis for an ever-expanding commercial empire. In Nigeria itself, the large Sindhi families, the Chanrais, the Chellerams and the Dalamals, controlled department stores, manufacturing and transport businesses. They were not generally liked. There is an old Indian proverb 'See a snake, see a Sindhi: kill the Sindhi.'

For such clever businessmen to involve themselves, as they so often did, in internecine family feuds, seemed completely ridiculous, even if it did provide marvellous business for my litigation department. The latest was between two brothers. My client wanted to obtain simultaneous freezing injunctions on his brother's ample assets in London, New York and Lagos. Maggie and I drew the short straw, and prepared to travel out to Lagos. The client sent

103

over the tickets at the last moment, and it was difficult to work out from which airport the plane was to take off. One of my partners, who had been there before, assured us it was Gatwick. We duly arrived there, and went up to the British Caledonian desk. 'Two for Lagos,' I said jocularly. 'You mean Lusaka,' was the reply.

My partner had been wrong. The flight left from Heathrow. We made a dash for it, missed our flight, and thus lost our day to acclimatise. The client met us off the plane at the gangway at Lagos, and ushered us easily through Immigration and Customs. His driver was clearly carrying what looked like a Colt 45, and I was glad that we had not been left to find our own way into town. Our host apologised that he could not get us into the Holiday Inn, the best hotel, as it was full for a conference, but we were to stay at the next best, the Federal Palace.

One look, and I renamed it the Feral Palace. The place stank. A combination of damp, decay, lack of ventilation and bad cooking produced an aroma enough to make you gag. We were warned not to take the lift, because of the frequent and unannounced power cuts. The purpose of the candles in the room, and the full bucket of water in the bathroom, were quite clear. I was surprised, when I went to use the bathroom in the middle of the night, to hear small chirping noises coming from the bucket. When I put on the light to investigate, I found two tiny frogs indulging in a complex mating ritual in our emergency water supply.

It had been dark when we had arrived, so I had not seen what was outside our window. The next morning I discovered that we overlooked a muddy bank on which a variety of items of garbage had been thrown. It was the same view from the picture windows of the dining room, where we ate our disgusting breakfast. The client came to collect us and, as we stewed in the scarcely moving and much polluting traffic, he told us of the government's latest efforts to free up the roads. They had passed a law that government employees, of which there was a legion, must only use their cars on alternate days, depending whether their licence plates ended in an odd or even number. The response had been a strike, which had only ended when the government issued a second car to each civil servant, so that they now had both odd and even number plates, and were able to revert to daily journeys in their cars.

We eventually reached the office of the local lawyers, only to find that they were utterly incompetent. The freezing injunction was at this stage unknown in Nigerian law, so we were about to make legal history. Maggie and I drafted the appropriate documents between us, and then had to supervise the typists, who seemed incapable of producing work which was not strewn with the most elementary errors. We paused for lunch, and the client took us to see his office, which was in an area where all the Sindhis operated. In London, they were notorious for their opulent homes, and to see here the abject squalor in which they made most of their money was a considerable shock. You had to cross an open sewer on a plank to reach what was little more than a wooden shack, albeit equipped with the latest office equipment and a sleek modern generator for when the mains supply failed.

We eventually had the papers ready, and rushed to court to appear before a black-robed judge, and obtain our injunction. Of course, we had no rights of audience, and had to use a local barrister to do the talking. Despite the fact that we had written out the script for him word for word, he nearly messed it up, and there was a lot of frantic tugging of his gown before the judge finally gave us what we wanted. The client was delighted, and immediately offered us the use of his bungalow up country for the weekend. I did not have to pause, or even look at Maggie, before I replied. 'Do you mind if we get the late night flight back to London, but thank you very much all the same?' We could not wait to get out of the place. We said goodbye to the client at the airport and were left to deal with the Emigration and Customs formalities by ourselves.

We joined a long queue, which moved slowly. By the time we reached the head, they were beginning to call our flight on the tannoy, which made us both extremely nervous. We found ourselves in front of a desk, at which sat an enormous official in full uniform. 'Where is your blue card?' he asked. 'I haven't got a blue card,' I replied. 'Show me your money then.' I produced my wallet, and he extracted two £20 notes, which he proceeded to slide into his back pocket. 'You go,' he commanded dismissively. I was opening and shutting my mouth like a recently landed fish. I wanted to protest, but I could hear on the tannoy the last call for our flight and the thought of spending the night arguing the toss in some small room at the airport was not attractive. We breathed a sigh of relief as we fastened our seat belts, and swore never to come back.

PART 2

Modupe Akintola was a woman with enormous powers of persuasion. Many years after my first trip to Nigeria, the International Bar Association (IBA) was putting together its biennial West African Forum, which was due to be held in Lagos. By now, I had become a regular and popular lecturer on the third-world circuit. A few years before in Durban, I had conducted a one-man question and answer session, which lasted almost the whole day. The president of the IBA had complained that not only was the room full, but so many people were queuing to get in that she could not get near. I still had no desire to repeat my triumph in Nigeria. Maggie was by now a world expert on the law of child abduction and she was firmly of the same opinion.

It was Modupe's gentle advocacy that finally persuaded us. A group of us travelled from London to be met by a large van with armed guards. It transpired that the road from the airport into Lagos was notorious for kidnapping. A prominent notice in our hotel room announcing that on no account should we agree to change any tour arrangements without first checking at the front desk did little to dispel the impression that the ransom business was alive and flourishing.

The next evening, we were taken to a performance of Stainer's *Crucifixion*, a work which was completely out of fashion in England. The fervour of the all-black cast of singers was extraordinary, and we could not help but be moved.

At the conference opening, we all helped with the registration formalities. Each delegate was to be provided with an extremely attractive red leather briefcase, but the organisers had reckoned without the Nigerian propensity to turn up at the last moment without prior registration and expect everything. There were about fifty last-minute delegates all clamouring for their briefcases, the supply of which had of course run out. They received short shrift from me.

The session went well, but we had a problem. The Chair of the Nigerian Children's Society was the wife of a prominent industrialist. She refused to leave Abuja, the country's capital. Maggie's session on child abduction came within her ambit. If Mohammed would not come to the mountain, then the mountain would have to go to Mohammed. Arrangements were made for the two of us to fly to Abuja. Fortunately, we were escorted to the national airport and onto the flight. Such was the indiscriminate chaos at that airport that I am sure we would never have made it on our own.

After the sticky, teeming tumult of Lagos, Abuja seemed like a ghost city. I have never seen an airport so far from its city. It must have been at least forty miles. Abuja was a mass of empty roads, flyovers and subways. There were huge office buildings, but no people. It was deliberately sited in the middle of the country between the Christian south and the Muslim north. The enormous cathedral was matched by the equally large mosque, but still the impression was that this was an almost empty city.

We checked into the Sheraton, and were shown to our room. I opened the door to find the room swarming with mosquitoes. I backed away hastily, and insisted that the room was thoroughly sprayed before we entered. I had no wish to return to England with malaria.

The next day, we presented ourselves early at the new, but deserted, conference centre. Time passed, including the scheduled starting time, and nobody appeared. Occasional faces looked round the door, saw only the two of us in the vast, banked arena, and disappeared. I was getting extremely angry at the discourtesy shown to Maggie. More than an hour had elapsed when we heard police sirens and two police motorcyclists arrived in a spray of gravel with sirens blaring, to be followed by a cavalcade of limousines with more police outriders bringing up the rear.

Out waddled a number of extremely fat ladies clad in spectacular and colourful native dress, who made their way into the building. This was the prominent industrialist's wife with her ladies in waiting. Eventually, they all seated themselves, and delegates suddenly appeared from all parts of the building where they had been hiding. I looked round to see that the room was now completely full. If I had thought that Maggie was now going to be asked to speak, I would have been wrong. The next hour and a half was filled with the most ridiculous exercise of protocol, in which the prominent industrialist's wife recognised each and every one of the self-important fishwives who accompanied her, and they in turn her.

By now, I was absolutely steaming, and it was almost a surprise and an anti-climax when Maggie was eventually called upon to speak. By contrast with the rubbish that had gone before, her presentation did not last long. After a few perfunctory questions, the prominent industrialist's wife rose to give a vote of thanks, and it quickly became obvious that she was virtually inarticulate and uneducated. She, in her turn, was thanked in an unctuous display of undeserved flattery by the woman who had organised the event, who had let slip, in an unguarded moment to us earlier, what she truly thought of the lady in question. The whole entourage then waddled out, like a line of ducks to their waiting cars, and the whole procession took off with sirens blaring and blue lights flashing.

We spent the next few days by the pool recovering, then flew back to London, vowing, again, never to return to that God-forsaken place and its people.

20

SRI LANKA AND ST TROPEZ

Hospitality and Good Fortune

Whenever we went on a trip, I always made a point of contacting the local lawyers. Sometimes, the results were instantaneous, but normally you had to wait before they needed a lawyer in London. Building up a practice was a slow business, and you had to look for opportunities in the most unlikely corners. Sadly, most of my partners did not share this need to market. I found out that one was planning to visit Los Angeles, so I asked him to visit a local lawyer, who was a friend. 'But I'm on holiday,' he replied plaintively. It was no wonder that I sometimes felt like a mother bird, trying to feed a bunch of fledgling cuckoos in the nest.

The ten-day Kuoni Sun tour to Sri Lanka seemed too cheap to be true. Kuoni was opening up a new market for the company. Maggie and I booked, then I wrote to the High Commissioner in London informing him that we were two English lawyers who wanted to meet local lawyers on our visit. He wrote back to say that he had delegated his nephew to look after us there. We flew overnight, and were transferred to our hotel. One of the reasons for the cheapness of the trip immediately became obvious. The Pegasus Reef Hotel was conveniently situated between the leper colony and the crippled children's home. The beach was covered with all sorts of debris, as it was opposite the port of Colombo. You swam in that sea at your peril. The terrace on which we took breakfast swarmed with flies. Nevertheless, we were enjoying ourselves. Ours was a lively and congenial group. We soon discovered that no one was married to his or her partner, so we renamed it the Kuoni Sin Tour.

The next morning, having forgotten all about the High Commissioner's letter, we were dressed for lounging by the pool when Mr Rodrigo called. He was impeccably dressed in a black coat and striped trousers. I do not know what his uncle had said, but he had put the fear of God into him. We managed to deflect him for the moment, but not before agreeing to a rigorous tour schedule for the rest of our time there. It turned out to be well worth it. I also had clients, the Hirdaramani family, who wanted to see us, so we were in for a busy ten days. The Hirdaramanis lived in great luxury with hordes of servants. This was perhaps why they were a little on the plump side. We had been upstairs to see the baby, and Maggie realised, when we had sat down again in the living room, that she had left her handbag in the nursery. She rose to get it, but was immediately urged to sit down, and a servant was dispatched to fetch it. Twenty minutes later, she was still waiting for it. They were extremely kind and hospitable people. We were beginning to feel like the rope in a tug of war as Mr Rodrigo would not let up.

He took us to Kandy, and after visiting the Temple of the Sacred Tooth, we had a very English tea in the rather dilapidated lounge of the Queen's Hotel. 'Would you like some more cakey?' asked the ancient waiter. I could not disappoint him. Mr Rodrigo then took us south to see the beautiful Bentota Beach, where there were wonderful hotels, so unlike our own. We visited Galle with its Dutch influence, and we had difficulty persuading Mr Rodrigo to take us back to the hotel, such was his enthusiasm.

We managed to reserve the next morning for sunbathing with the group. I was lying there baking, as the sun was extremely hot, even through seemingly thick clouds, when a pageboy brought me a fax. 'Congratulations', it said, 'you have won first prize in the Annabel's Xmas Raffle'. As I have never won anything in my life, partly because I rarely enter raffles, I thought it had to be a hoax, then I remembered that, on my last day in the office, a particularly insistent client had telephoned and sold me a raffle ticket for £25, a huge sum in those days. I doubt whether I would have bought it at all, but I was keen to get him off the line, so that I could clear my desk before departing on the trip. As I had forgotten my cheque-book that day, I drew one on the office, and sent it off to him in the post. I still thought that it was a hoax. The prize was a new Riva Speedboat, allegedly worth £7,000. I was hardly in the league to need it. Another fax then came from the client confirming my win, and reminding me that the prize also included a week's stay for two at the Byblos Hotel in St Tropez in order to receive the prize.

After buying a few celebratory rounds, we were ready for Mr Rodrigo, but I was still thinking what to do about the boat, considering the astronomical annual cost of maintaining, insuring and mooring a boat of this type. I was then in the midst of a messy divorce battle with Judy, my first wife, and needed all the money I could raise to pay off the builders who had worked on the house into which we had moved, only for me to move out almost immediately. I realised that, as a divorce lawyer, I was setting a very bad example. It was a question of do as I say, rather than do as I do.

Mr Rodrigo announced that we were going to take tea with the Chief Abbott of the Buddhist monks. The Singhalese seemed an extremely lazy people, and to be a monk looked to me to be a particularly lazy existence, as the people fed and clothed you. All the work was done by the Tamils, who were a very industrious people. At that time, the local newspapers were full of the strike of the Tamil 'toddy tappers'. Toddy was an extremely strong local spirit distilled from the sap of the coconut palm. To extract it, the Tamil toddy tapper had to climb the smooth trunk of the palm tree aided by a short rope tied between his legs, cut the bark and wait for the sap to fill the metal cup which he held. He then reversed down the tree. I learned how every part of the coconut palm had some lucrative use. The smell of it certainly pervaded our hotel room, as all the furniture was polished with its oil, which was also used extensively in cooking.

After a most interesting tour of the monastery campus and buildings, we were ushered into a room to await the Abbott. He arrived with a swirl of his saffron robes. He was extremely tall, thin and, of course, bald. His English was perfect. I remarked on the fact as he poured the tea. 'It should be.' he replied. 'I spent three years at King's College, London, reading for a maths degree.'

That night Mr Rodrigo was to take us to a Perera in Colombo. We knew about the Perera in Kandy from our guidebooks. It was a night-time procession of more than one hundred and fifty elephants, but this was the wrong time of year. Mr Rodrigo took us to his house and, after a superb meal, we were seated on virtual thrones in the front of his garden overlooking the roadside. We felt like British royalty attending some durbar or jamboree in India. The music sounded discordant to our ears, as the first elephant appeared. We were very well protected, but everywhere else there were undisciplined throngs of people. The darkness was intermittently illuminated with torches held by bystanders, but the elephants were lit from trunk to tail by coloured fairy lights like Christmas trees. It was an incredible sight. A thick cable was attached to the tail of each elephant, and the cable in turn was linked to an electricity generator standing on a lorry, which slowly followed each elephant. This was a combined triumph of ancient ceremony and modern technology.

Groups of dancers, jugglers, fire-eaters and other entertainers filled the gaps between the processing elephants, and the bands were making a tremendous din. Maggie happened to express delight at the performance of a particular group of dancers. Mr Rodrigo immediately dispatched a servant to run after them and bring them back to perform specially for us on the lawn. We felt very privileged, but were getting extremely tired. There must have been at least fifty elephants. Eventually, Mr Rodrigo dropped us off at the hotel, and we rushed into the bar to tell the other members of the group about the Perera. They took taxis to try to find it, but failed. I think they thought we were making it up.

The next day was Christmas Day, which coincided with a strike of all the hotel staff except the senior management. Christmas dinner was accordingly much delayed. We compensated by drinking a lot, which was just as well, as the turkey curry, when it at last arrived, was the hottest thing that any of us had ever eaten. We sat there with tears rolling down our faces. Whether this was done as sabotage by a disgruntled head chef, or sheer inexperience by a manager turned chef for the night, we never found out.

We were due to fly back on Boxing Day, but the plane was delayed. The tour manager was apologising profusely, but the whole group was delighted at the prospect of an extra night's holiday. We were transferred to the Galle Face Hotel in Colombo, which was a relic of our colonial past. The bedrooms were all off open verandas, where white-clad servants slept all night. Air conditioning was unknown, and we shared our room with a horde of hungry mosquitoes. We sat in the dining room in enormous wicker-backed chairs, which creaked loudly at every movement. The visitors' book in the still elegant, though run-down, hotel jewellers told an interesting tale of the past. Colombo had been a coaling station for the ocean-going liners on the way to Australia and everybody who was anybody had stopped at the hotel and bought jewellery in the shop, from the Queen downwards.

We were sad to leave Sri Lanka, though many of the group became long-term friends and clients. I had immediately to deal with the situation of my raffle win, which had attracted national press publicity. Judy's lawyers had already written asking for a share of the proceeds of sale of the boat. I paid the firm back the cost of the raffle ticket, but this did not stop my partners from demanding their shares of the boat. I said to them, 'If I had won a turkey, would you have wanted a drumstick?' I won the argument, but there was a residue of bitterness remaining among them.

Maggie and I now made arrangements to drive down to St Tropez to receive our prize. I had lunch with Mark Birley, the proprietor of Annabel's, to make the arrangements. He assured me that the hotel deposit had been paid, and the bill would be taken care of. I was driving a rather brutal Ford Capri with a three-litre engine. The previous year, it had broken down at the autoroute toll at Villefranche Sur Saone. It broke down again on this journey at precisely the same place.

We eventually arrived at the Hotel Byblos in St Tropez and stepped into another world. The British property boom was at its height, and most of the top developers and investors seemed to be staying at the Byblos. There were lines of Bentleys, Aston Martins and Jensens with British number plates parked outside. I thankfully parked my car in the hotel garage. Our room was on two levels and superb. In fact, the whole hotel was superb. When you telephoned to place your order for breakfast in your room in the morning, I swear that you had hardly put down the receiver when there was a knock on the door, and a charming waiter was standing there with your tray. The place was completely informal, including the notice in the dining room, which said 'ties must *not* be worn in the dining room'. The disco was magnificent, and stayed open as long as we wanted it.

Soothing classical music played all day by the pool, in the middle of which was a platform, which was usually occupied by a beautiful woman sitting cross-legged and topless while rhythmically oiling her breasts with sun-screen to the sounds of a Bach fugue. It was difficult to drag your eyes from the sight. Among the many distinguished people staying there were Prince Charles and the Parker-Bowles. We knew nothing of their subsequent history, but they seemed an awkward threesome. I felt sorry for the plain clothes detectives trying to make themselves inconspicuous among the palm trees, sweltering in their tweed sports jackets which they needed to cover the side arms that they were obviously carrying.

We were joined by a friend of mine, Brian Rutland and his group, who were also staying in St Tropez. Frankly, after the Byblos, the rest of St Tropez was rather tawdry and an anti-climax, and we rushed back to its comfort after every excursion. Brian was not only a successful property developer, but also an expert on boats, and I wanted his opinion. We walked down to the boatyard and a little man came out to greet us. 'I've come about the Annabel's boat,' I said. He at first looked blank, then light dawned. 'Ah, the Annabel's boat. You must first pay the storage charges,' and he fished out and gave me a bill of several thousand francs. 'I'm not going to pay this now,' I said, 'but can we see it?' 'No,' he replied, 'it's not here.' I still wanted to know more, and saw a rather sleek-looking boat in the showroom behind. 'Is it as big as that'? I asked. It looked enormous to me. 'No,' he answered, 'yours is bigger.' We were clearly getting nowhere, so we returned to the safety of the Byblos, and I could digest the news that I was the owner of a big boat, which was eating up storage charges, and which I could not see.

Our week was up, and it was time to go. Our bags were taken from the room, and I went to the front desk to say goodbye to the receptionist, whom we had got to know quite well. I moved to shake hands with him, and was left with a piece of paper in my hand. It was a bill for an enormous sum. I examined it, and saw that credit had been given for a deposit paid by Annabel's, but there was no denying the evidence that we had spent a lot. I explained to the manager, who by now had joined the receptionist, that this bill was not for me, but was to be paid by Annabel's. He replied gently, but firmly, to the effect that those were not his instructions, and that I must pay the bill. The debate continued, but I could see that I was losing. With as much good grace as I could summon under the circumstances, I fished out a Diners Card, which was accepted. My already ravaged finances were now even more in tatters.

The porters brought our luggage to the car, and I ostentatiously did not tip them. The car was loaded and I switched on the engine. Nothing! In the week that it had sat there, the battery had gone completely flat. It was Saturday afternoon, and I could not find a garage open anywhere. In the end, I had to crawl back to the hotel desk and ask for help. They soon found a mechanic, and we departed with me bestowing lavish tips all round.

A second lunch with Mark Birley in London ensured that everything due was properly paid, but I failed in any attempt to persuade him to fund a return trip, on the basis of the nervous shock that we had suffered as a result of our terrible treatment. He did not take me seriously, nor frankly did I myself. As for the Riva speedboat,

I sold it without ever seeing it. I felt like an unmarried mother putting her child out for adoption without actually seeing the child for fear that, if she did, she would be unable to part with it. The boat was sold as though second-hand, and I did not receive all that much for it after paying the broker's commission. Nevertheless, it went some way to pay off the more pressing of my debts. Who was I to look a gift boat in the mouth?

21

GHANA

Warmest of Welcomes and Educating Samuel

I always seemed to have some kind of connection with Ghana. When I joined Anthony Sumption in 1961, his client, Humphry Berkeley, was suing the *Sunday Express* for calling him Nkrumah's lackey. I took over the action, which settled eventually on satisfactory terms. During the course of preparing for trial, I interviewed a retired white lawyer, John Lynes, who had made his life in Ghana, and I was immensely impressed by his passion for the place and the people. Whites generally were being kicked out of the country, but he was determined to stay.

The next great contact was through Khow Amiyiah, who met one of my partners at a Territorial Army meeting, and was passed to me to act as his lawyer. Amiyiah had been President Nkrumah's chief of security. There had been a big falling out between them, and Amiyiah had fled to a nearby African country, from where Nkrumah had tried unsuccessfully to extradite him. Afterwards, he had settled in London, but he was always plotting to return.

He had asked me to call in and see him on my way home one sunny evening. He had a flat on the Cromwell Road. I parked beside a large television news lorry, from which thick, black cables snaked across the pavement to the front door of the flat, which was open. I went in to find Amiyiah, a very big man, looking extremely handsome in a white suit, standing before the camera and explaining how he had given the coded signal for his supporters in Ghana to rise up and overthrow the then president, General Acheompong.

117

He was now going back to his home country to take over as its new ruler. This interview appeared later that evening on television news, and caused a considerable sensation.

Amiyiah told me that his supporters in London had no money, and asked if I could help raise the air fares for their return. I had recently lunched with clients, the directors of a small city merchant bank, who told me that they were looking for contacts to provide economic advice to developing countries. I took Amiyiah along to see them, and they agreed to fund the trip for Amiyiah and a group of his supporters in consideration of his procuring a contract to give economic advice to the country, once he had taken control.

A few weeks later, I happened to be watching the late-night news, and I was shocked to see pictures of Amiyiah, still wearing the same white suit, standing on a kitchen chair with an equally large Askari pointing a rifle at his head. Amiyiah recanted completely, and confirmed that it was not his revolution at all. My banking clients had lost their money. I heard that he was in jail in Ghana, and I never expected to see him again. I was pleasantly surprised when he breezed into my office eighteen months later, but looking a shadow of his former self. He had lost a great deal of weight. Having been let out, anyone else would have learned a lesson to interfere no further in Ghanaian politics, but not Amiyiah.

He wanted to provoke an armed uprising, but this meant purchasing the arms. The world of arms dealing is not one with which I was familiar, and I went along with the proposal out of curiosity, convinced that it was an academic exercise only, as Amiyiah would never be able to raise the funds. We were entertained in an extremely luxurious office in Mayfair by sober-suited individuals who looked and behaved like bankers and wore Guards or Old Etonian ties. We were presented with glossy brochures containing a two-part tariff. The cheaper price list was for established governments and consisted of every possible item from boots and gaiters to heavy artillery and tanks. The other part consisted of the same items, but at double the cost. I queried this, and it was explained to me that revolutionaries always had to pay at least double. Amiyiah made a shopping list of his requirements for his revolution, and we then discussed delivery.

It was considered far too risky by the arms dealers to deliver the goods on the beaches of Ghana, and it was agreed that they would be consigned to tramp steamers, which would anchor offshore at designated times and dates, waiting for Amiyiah's people to come out from the land by boat to collect. The deal was agreed very smoothly, subject only to the prior provision of the money on our side. On this occasion, my confidence that it would not be forthcoming proved correct. I was very amused, in general conversation over coffee afterwards, to be told that the lawyers who acted for the arms dealers were one of the top four City of London firms. Somehow, it seemed totally appropriate.

Amiyiah disappeared from my life for a time. When he reappeared, it was at the height of the war between Nigeria and Biafra, in which he had been fighting on the Biafran side, but they were now losing. However, he had the answer to the problem. We, which presumably included me, were going to buy a large military aeroplane and bomb Lagos! In a long professional career I have had many crazy proposals put to me, but this one took the biscuit. Fortunately, Amiyiah again had no means of raising the money, and that was the last I saw of him.

I had always wanted to visit Ghana. I had a number of other Ghanaian clients, and they always seemed so cheerful and friendly, unlike their Nigerian counterparts, whose country I never wanted to see again. The opportunity arose once more through the International Bar Association, which was organising the biennial West African Lawyers' congress in Accra. I was asked to go out to speak, and I was happy to accept the invitation. Accra was so unlike Lagos. There was no feeling of threat or menace, and the small group of us, who had come out to lecture, could wander anywhere with impunity. At the weekend, the beach became a very sticky and steamy playground. The whole population seemed to be out enjoying itself.

Not surprisingly, the city was somewhat run-down, but the

Conference Centre was a revelation. The interior was clad in a mixture of beautiful, polished African woods, and it was a privilege to speak in it. The delegates came from all over Africa. I was surprised to learn that the quickest way to fly from Addis Ababa to Accra, not a long journey as the crow flies, was via Heathrow.

After a long and tiring day's session, I was in the mood for some entertainment. Our hotel had something called a 'jazz bar', but none of our group would accompany me. They all wanted an early night, so I went in on my own. The music was not jazz, and I was the only hotel guest. The bar was packed with local prostitutes, but they cheerfully accepted the fact that I was not looking for business. For the price of a few drinks and some food for the hungry girls, I learned a lot about conditions in Ghana. Elementary education was provided free by the State, but secondary school had to be paid for, and few families were in a position to fund their children. For the rest of the trip, I used to call in for a nightcap every evening. On my last night, I announced that I was leaving the next day and I was escorted by a guard of honour of the girls, as far as the door leading to the residential part of the hotel, but no further.

The gala dinner at the end of the conference took place around the pool. All the delegates wore their native dress, and it made a wonderful and variegated sight of so many colours. The problem was that it was stiflingly hot and humid in the open air, and the Europeans found it intolerable. The next evening, I was invited to dinner by an old Cambridge friend, whom I had contacted. In fact, I had used his law firm over the years for assistance on a number of occasions. Johnnie Quashie Idun had been a great singer and guitarist at Cambridge. He formed a duo with Rory McEwan in the Footlights, and I can still see his smiling face, as he formed part of the rhythm section of a very good university jazz band. John told me about his life in Ghana. He had a few regrets, and he told me how, at the time of graduating, his father was putting pressure on him to return to Ghana and join the family law firm. He received an invitation to go to New York to audition for a part in a new, all-black musical, but he returned to Ghana instead. The part went to a newcomer, Harry Belafonte, and Johnnie was left for the rest of his life to ponder on how different his existence might have been if he had attended the audition and got the part.

The local lawyers were extremely hospitable, and arranged for us to have a tour by minibus of as much of the country as we could see in a day. We visited an extraordinary game reserve and nature park, where progress was made along very narrow, swaying, wooden bridges, anchored from one tree to another, situated high above the valleys below. There were any number of these, and the problem was that, once you had started you had to continue, as there was no means of going back. I was not the only one with no head for heights, and this part of the trip was an ordeal. The idea was to look down at the beauty below. For me, this was impossible.

There was a great deal of poverty in Accra, but nothing to what we saw in the countryside. Rusty corrugated iron seemed to be the building material of choice, and open ditches by the side of the mud streets were their substitute for drains. The roads were rutted and pitted to such an extent that we were bounced around like dice in a cup.

The Cape Coast was a revelation. Beautiful white sands, cooled by ocean breezes, abundant swaying palm trees, but positively no infrastructure. To this day, I dream of finding some imaginative billionaire to fund the roads, airport, power, sewage and other amenities to turn this place into a playground for rich Europeans, whose money could do so much to transform the lives of these lovely people. The flight would be little more than four hours, and there would be no jet lag, as the longitude is almost the same as that of Europe.

We reached Elmina, where we visited a Portuguese slave fort. Our guide did little to diminish our western, middle-class guilt. The whitewashed building had an elegance which contrasted with the purpose to which it was put. We were shown the relatively small rooms, where male and female slaves were packed separately like sardines, waiting for the ships to come and carry them off to the New World. The fort was built by the sea, so that the ships could come alongside, and the slaves merely had to step out of an opening on to the deck of the waiting ship. It was difficult not to let my imagination run riot.

On the way out, we were accosted by a group of raggedly dressed small boys. One thrust a card into my hand, which contained his name and address. He asked me to send him a postcard from England. His name was Samuel Kwofie, and this was the start of a long relationship. I sent him the promised postcard, and our correspondence developed. It was not long before he asked me to pay for his secondary education. Knowing what I knew then, £20 a term did not seem much.

The bills gradually increased in size, and by the end I was paying £200 per term at a residential technical college for Samuel to graduate as a refrigeration and air conditioning engineer. At one stage, Samuel was informally adopted by my whole office. He was changing schools, and he sent me a list of his requirements. He wanted training shoes, so he sent me a tracing of his feet. I put the list on the office intranet, and was inundated with calculators, cameras, watches and everything which was so precious to him, but is so taken for granted by us. It was all parcelled up and sent out to him, but to this day I do not know if it actually reached him. I fear someone intercepted the package.

Over the years, I supplied textbooks, which seemed virtually unobtainable in Ghana, together with a mobile phone. When Samuel graduated, he asked me to bring him to England, so that he could live with his family, including his 'brothers', as he called my children. At this stage, I had to be tough. I told him that I had paid for his education so that he could be of benefit to his own country. When he had saved up enough from working to buy a ticket to London, I would happily sponsor a holiday visit, but I had seen too many Africans, after being well educated, leave their homes, and make their new life in Europe or America, thus defeating one of the main objects of the exercise. I am not sure that he appreciated my philosophy, but he had to accept it.

22

GABON

Do Not Believe All You Are Told

I never thought that I would have the chance to work in the French speaking part of Africa, if only because my command of the language was so poor. I had had an excellent education in written French, but perfunctory attention only was paid to oral skills. I could get by on holiday, but little more, and my skills in the language were diminishing, in contrast to my improving Italian, which was required if I was successfully to enjoy life in a second home in a remote village in the Tuscan foothills.

The client in this case, also an Indian, was introduced by Mr Shah of Kenya fame. He had been told of the success of my efforts in relation to the coffee smuggling case, and he now wanted me to turn my attention to a casino in Gabon. He opened his briefcase and drew out a sheaf of brightly coloured, bearer share certificates, which he told me represented seventy five per cent of the issued capital of the company, which owned and ran the main casino in Gabon and of which he was the unencumbered proprietor. Without his consent, false directors had been appointed in his absence, and he wanted me to attend the forthcoming annual general meeting, vote out the false directors and appoint new ones on a list, which he handed me. For unspecified reasons, he was unable to visit Gabon. I was not sure that he could even leave England.

With a substantial deposit on account of costs, the job seemed feasible, and Maggie and I could fly out on Thursday, attend the meeting on Friday, spend a leisurely weekend there, and return on Monday. We were told that our hotel account would be settled by the casino.

I was extremely interested in the contrasts between British and French Africa, which seemed to be largely down to sex. The British could have black mistresses, but they were discouraged from inter-marriage by the violent disapproval of the white wives living there. The French, by contrast, suffered no such inhibition. As a result, the British remained a ruling class apart, and when the former colonies gained their independence, in general had to leave, and British power and influence disappeared. The French, by inter-marriage, created subjects who considered themselves as French, so that, when their countries became independent, they remained tied voluntarily to France, sent deputies to the French Assembly, and still traded almost exclusively with France, using a currency tied to the French franc. I remembered hearing the President of the Ivory Coast speaking, when I was in Mauritius, in perfect and mellifluous French with the red ribbon of the Legion d'Honneur proudly displayed on his lapel. I wanted to see for myself how it worked.

We flew to Paris, and changed on to Air Gabon's sole Boeing 747, with the country's livery proudly displayed on its fuselage. The flight was almost empty, and we arrived to sudden darkness. Like all places near the Equator, twilight scarcely exists. The hotel was not particularly special, but we slept well, especially as there was no jet lag. One unpleasant surprise occurred when we were checking into the hotel. I was asked the usual question as to how I intended to pay. I replied, as instructed by the client, that our bill should be charged to the casino account. We were marched in to see the duty manager, and I was informed that this was not possible. I therefore reluctantly proffered my credit card.

The next day, we went down to the casino for the meeting. The room was packed. When the chairman called for shareholders to identify themselves I waved my bundle in the air, but so did many other people from all parts of the room. The company secretary, seated at a desk, slowly and laboriously took down details of the holders and numbers of the bearer shares. As he progressed, it became clear that the client had nothing like seventy five per cent, and his holding in fact was considerably less than ten per cent. The business of the meeting continued, and the hostile directors were re-appointed. There was nothing that we could do to prevent it. My newly-polished French (I had been working hard on it during the flight) was not put to use.

We had a great sense of anti-climax, and I sent an urgent fax to the client in London explaining what had happened. I ended with the words, 'wasting our time, and your money. Shall we come home?' If we stayed, it would be at our own expense in all probability, but I had to have the client's approval. The reply came quickly: 'come home'. We had time for one long walk along the endless beach, the sand of which had a strange greenish hue, before taking the taxi back to the airport. We bought, while we were waiting for our flight, some interesting stone figures, but that was the sum total of our experience of Gabon. On our return, the client asked me what I thought of the place. 'I don't know, I didn't see much of it,' I replied.

23

HONG KONG

Hectic, Exciting, but Ultimately Destructive

However hard I tried, I found it difficult to take Hong Kong seriously. Everything was so easy to achieve, and approached in a spirit of positivism and optimism. This contrasted so much with gloomy old London, where it was always so difficult to get anything done, where obstacles were always put in your way, and an atmosphere of defeatism, cynicism and pessimism almost always prevailed. The way in which Hong Kong changed people also worried me. Marriages were under threat, and often broke down under the strain. Timid introverts became raging extroverts overnight, and alcohol, gambling and drugs were everyday currency.

I first went as a tourist for three days in the early seventies, on one of those whistle-stop tours of the Far East, which could have been entitled 'if it's Tuesday, it must be Singapore'. I managed to cram in a few visits to law firms, but no important contacts were made, although I did receive a few Christmas cards. My abiding memory is freezing at the top of The Peak in clothes packed for the tropical weather, which we experienced everywhere else on the trip.

The next visit was some ten years later, and was very much a marketing trip. The offices of most of the law firms in Hong Kong are conveniently close together, and with good planning you could visit two an hour. I was politely received for a statutory thirty minutes on each visit. It seemed that tours from London law firms were an everyday occurrence. The difficulty was in differentiating myself from the pack.

I eventually struck oil with Fairbairn and Kwok, a mixed English and Chinese firm, of good reputation locally, which shared my expansionist philosophy. The senior partner, Martin Fairbairn, seemed to be my mirror image, and we were both keen to establish a close association, as we could see great opportunities for sharing work, which would enhance our respective practices. His partner, Willie Kwok, by contrast, was a well-connected local playboy. He showed me his immaculate office, where his desk bore not a scrap of paper. His work was done in the night clubs, where he met clients, and introduced them to the other lawyers in the firm to do the work.

That evening, Maggie and I were collected from our hotel by Willie in his Rolls-Royce, accompanied by his mistress, Felicity. His wife and children stayed at home. He regaled us with stories of his time as a barman at the Hilton in Park Lane, while he was studying for his law finals. At the disco, he was very much true to form, and was huddled with various groups of Chinese men. At one stage he broke away to come over to Maggie: 'Felicity is bored, please dance with her.' Maggie obliged.

I left Hong Kong with a close association between our two firms in the bag, a clutch of new clients, and an enormous file, on which I had to start work immediately. By publicising the association, I was able to attract new work from the type of clients who would previously have been out of our league. The clients out of Hong Kong were a very mixed lot, and often consisted of expatriates who had fled the UK for good or bad reasons, but retained interests here. Some of those in the textile trade were a little difficult to handle, and I soon realised that professional standards in Hong Kong were much more lax than in London. I had to re-educate some of the clients. One particular couple came to see me with a large briefcase, which was placed on my desk. 'Bung 'im, Jay,' was the command. The briefcase was opened to reveal wads of high denomination bank notes. They were both astonished when I insisted on counting and writing out a receipt for the money. Not to play it straight would have been the first step on a slippery slope, especially with those two.

On one occasion, one of them asked me as a special favour to deliver his monthly maintenance, which was in arrears, to his former wife. I was heading in that direction anyway, so I stopped off at a basement flat in Chelsea. Dolores was an American ex-model, and she had obviously already started on the evening's drinking. She insisted on making me a strawberry daiquiri. Unfortunately, she had not fastened the lid on the mixer, and the contents shot all over the kitchen, leaving strawberry stalactites hanging from the ceiling. She told me that, during her divorce, she had never paid any of her lawyers, but had slept with all of them. I believed her. I left for my next appointment with the smell of strawberry daiquiri in my hair.

Martin and I agreed to make our association still closer by establishing parallel firms in our respective countries, and exchanging partners. Martin and Bill Catley were already English solicitors with practising certificates, so there was no problem. It was necessary for us to go out to Hong Kong to be formally admitted to practise there. When we arrived, we were faced with the news that Willie Kwok had absconded to Taiwan with substantial client funds and that the firm had changed its name by excluding his from the title. I would not say this was treated as an everyday occurrence, but somehow it was not considered the catastrophe it would have been in London. We duly appeared in court one Saturday morning before the Chief Justice, Sir Denys Roberts, and a berobed Martin Fairbairn said nice things about us. We signed the roll and that was it. Not surprisingly, although I was now a Hong Kong lawyer, I never had the temerity to practise there, bearing in mind my lack of knowledge of the local laws.

A party was organised to celebrate our 'marriage'. In some respects, Hong Kong still does things very formally, and we had to stand interminably on the receiving line as our guests arrived. I broke protocol by becoming engaged in conversation at length with Piers Jacobs, who had been in my class at school, and whom I had not seen since then. He had risen to be Financial Secretary in the government. Frankly, while I enjoyed visiting Hong Kong for a week, I never felt that I wanted to spend longer there, and I would never have considered living there, even though it seemed such an easy place to make money, which could be retained because of the low level of taxation. An atmosphere of fear pervaded the place. Everybody seemed to be available for work around the clock and seven days a week. Hong Kong is the ideal jumping-off ground to visit all the wonderful places in the Pacific, but, as I talked to people, I realised that they rarely travelled, except on business, as they were afraid of leaving their desks and losing business opportunities as a result.

At home, the news of our Hong Kong links was becoming more widely known. I was asked to advise a young barrister in London who was having difficulty finding chambers and was thinking of making a fresh start as a lawyer in the government service in Hong Kong. He was very much a left-wing idealist, but, despite that fact, I thought he could do well there. The clinching question was when I asked him if he liked sailing.

He followed the normal practice of working for a year for the government, and then set up as a practising barrister, and did extremely well. He and his then family came to stay with us one summer in Italy. The two of us were sitting one early evening on a beautiful, deserted beach, watching a spectacular sunset. 'Michael,' he suddenly exclaimed, 'I want to talk about my investments.' 'Charlie,' I replied, 'to hell with your investments.' Hong Kong had succeeded in changing the idealistic left-winger into a rabid capitalist.

Another of the partners in the Hong Kong firm hit professional difficulties in relation to clients' money. I might have thought that our tie-up was particularly unfortunate, if news had not been received at about the same time that the senior partner of one of the largest and most reputable law firms in Hong Kong had been found face down and very dead in his swimming pool wearing a cement waistcoat. I had recently had direct dealings with him in his capacity of President of the Hong Kong Law Society. Otherwise I could not claim responsibility for his demise, even though he had disappointed me.

The years passed, and the links between our two firms became much more institutionalised and less personal. Although I was always pleased to see Martin as a friend, I was no longer involved in doing any of their work, and had passed it on to another partner. Professionally, our paths diverged, as my approach to clients was much more conservative. Martin was always trying to sell complex tax avoidance schemes, which worried me. I took the view that if I could not understand the scheme in three minutes, and could not explain it to the client in words of one syllable, it would not have my support. His love life was also at a critical stage. He had married his Chinese secretary, Amy, and she had left the firm to have his two children. He was now in love with his new Chinese secretary, Esther. Amy divorced him, and took him so much to the cleaners financially that he had to leave Hong Kong and set up a new life in London with Esther.

By chance, this coincided with my leaving my old firm, so I only learned about events at second hand. While he stayed as a consultant with my former firm, he opened his own office with new partners in very smart premises in Knightsbridge. Unfortunately, the combination of Amy's demands in Hong Kong, the lifestyle expectations of Esther in London, and a vicious recession, were too much for Martin's personal and professional integrity. He plundered the estate of a deceased airline pilot, of which he was executor, fled the country, and was struck off as a solicitor in England.

What is it about Hong Kong? Is it something in the air?

24

SARDINIA

How to Lose Money in Glamorous Surroundings

I almost always found it difficult acting for clients in the pop music business. Far too often, the managers and agents were rogues, while the artistes were fools. The managers introduced the artistes, so it was the latter who were the clients. As the lawyer, you soon discovered that the managers were robbing the artistes in some way. Your professional duty was quite clear, but your commercial interests told you the opposite. The artistes came and went, while you relied on the managers for the flow of new clients. Offend the managers at your peril. I preferred not to be involved.

I did act for the lead singer of a well-known rock group, but not in matters relating to the music business. He and his family had been persuaded to put up the money for a venture to run a ferry service between Sardinia and Corsica. He was by no means a fool, and I was never able to find out by what flight of fantasy he had been inveigled into making a substantial investment in a project on which he had done no research, and where his knowledge of the subject matter was virtually nil.

The ferries in question were Russian-built hydrofoils of a modern design. They had been used effectively on Lake Baikal and the Caspian Sea, but nowhere else. They had been specially built at great expense, and then transported to Sardinia, but there for the moment the trail ended. My client had been trying in vain to find out what had happened to the project in general, and the boats in particular. His so-called partner in the proposed service had disappeared, and he was not helped by the fact that he did not speak a word of Italian.

I agreed to go out with Maggie to try to sort out the mess. As we needed an Italian lawyer as well, whom we could trust, the client agreed that I should ask my lawyer friend in Grosseto, Giorgio Padovani, to fly out and join us for the latter part of the trip. The hydrofoils had been shipped to Olbia near the Costa Smeralda, so that was to be the starting point of our trip.

I left the flight details to the travel agents, and Maggie and I flew out on a late evening flight to Alghero. We had arranged a booking at the Hotel Pitrizza on the Costa Smeralda, so I gave the name of the hotel and the town, Olbia, to the taxi driver. He roared with laughter. 'It will take you five hours to get there and cost you a fortune. You have come to the wrong airport!' It was already nearly midnight, so we had to cut our losses for the moment. We found a hotel for the night, and next day we went to the local Avis office and hired a self-drive car. The drive across the northern part of Sardinia was breathtaking. The roads were windy and empty of other vehicles. The scenery consisted of wild moorlands with misty mountains in the background. There were abundant clumps of purple heather and bright yellow gorse. For a landscape artist, it would have been paradise. On one stop by the roadside, I was stupid enough to try to pick a prickly pear off one of the many cactuses. I learned to my cost why they were so named, and for several hours found it difficult to grip the steering wheel because of the pain caused by the almost invisible spines which had lodged in my flesh. The villages and towns seemed shuttered and deserted as we drove through. I learned much later that this was bandit country, where the local hobby was kidnapping foreigners for ransom. We were lucky that it was the bandits' day off.

We stopped for lunch at what looked like an upmarket log cabin. The smell of wood smoke from the blazing fire perfumed the air. The food was fresh and extremely good. The wafer-like unleavened bread was particularly tasty. The waiters fell about laughing when I ordered fennel in Italian. I did not know that the Italian word for it, '*finnochio*', is also slang for 'gay', which the waiters were to a man.

As the taxi driver prophesised, the journey did take five hours. Olbia turned out to be a rather shabby port town, but the Costa Smeralda was like a fairy-tale come to life. At first sight, Porto Cervo was an ancient fishing port. All the buildings were harmoniously painted in faded and muted colours. The effect was beautiful, especially in the rays of the setting sun. It was only as we entered the town that we saw that everything was recently built to a very clever architectural design to simulate the appearance of an antique fishing port. The whole area had been a mosquito-ridden swamp, which was virtually uninhabitable. The marshes had been drained and the area developed for high-class tourism by the Aga Khan, employing exclusively British expertise.

We still had some way to go to reach the Hotel Pitrizza. When we arrived it was beautifully situated and built in a modern style. The rooms were white-walled bungalows with a stippled finish dotted among the semi-tropical grounds. The only problem was that we were sharing our room with any number of mosquitoes. I went on safari with a knotted towel, and by the time I had finished the walls were no longer pristine white, but covered with blotches, which were all too often red, showing that the mosquitoes had been able to draw first blood before meeting their untimely death.

The next morning, we dragged ourselves away from the beautiful infinity pool to begin our quest. In a small port town, where not much happens, the arrival of four Russian hydrofoils had been an event. The problem was that our client's partner had overlooked the question of Customs' formalities. As a result, the boats had been impounded by Customs for non-payment of duty, and now sat in a compound paradoxically situated on a hilltop. We were taken to see them, and sure enough there they sat in pristine condition. To put them on a hilltop seemed a very Irish solution to the problem, and I was not surprised to learn that Sardinia is to Italy as Ireland is to the British mainland. There are many Italian jokes about the strange habits of the locals.

We next did some research about the proposed ferry service

between Sardinia and Corsica. The results were not propitious. This was a particularly stormy strait, and the hydrofoils were designed for much calmer seas, and hence were entirely unfit for the purpose. With some local help, I was able to do a quick calculation. The Customs duty, interest and storage charges were a large and ever-increasing sum. The second-hand value of the hydrofoils, albeit still in excellent condition, was far less, and depreciating. Add into the equation the expense of transporting the boats to a place where they could be useful, and it quickly became clear that I had to tell the client that he had lost his investment and should cut his losses.

There was still the question of the joint bank account in the name of the client and his former partner. I had no authority to ask, but I thought it worth visiting the bank to try to find out what was in the account. Imagine my astonishment when they told me the balance figure without any hesitation, or even checking my credentials. The rules of banking secrecy became a little stretched in the remote island of Sardinia. Unfortunately, it was not a sum of money enough to make the client's day.

Giorgio now arrived, and I had to tell him that he was here only for playtime and not for work. The poolside of the Pitrizza was extremely cosmopolitan. Giorgio had always played the typical Italian ladies' man, but here he met his match. He was set upon by an archetypal Jewish American princess, who pursued him every-where. He swore to us that she groped him in the swimming pool. We were falling about with laughter, and bets were being placed as to whether, like the Royal Canadian Mounted Police, she would get her man.

The drive back to Alghero was equally memorable. This time it was Sunday, and all the towns and villages were *en fête*. The people were dressed in their best clothes, and slowly promenading up and down the main, and often only, street. This made it difficult for us in our car. To hoot, or otherwise seek to hurry them, would have been unthinkable. We just had to go slowly with the flow. Every-body noted our presence, and was extremely good humoured towards us, but there was clearly an etiquette which we had to observe. Like a convoy, we moved at the speed of the slowest.

The client was very philosophical about his loss. I think he knew deep down that the situation was hopeless, but he just wanted to be sure. As to the hydrofoils, I assume that they still sit to this day on their Sardinian hilltop, as a monument to the continuing gullibility of mankind.

25

PARIS MATCH

Chauvinism at its Worst

His Royal Highness Prince Mohamed Bolkiah of Brunei was a great client to have. I acted for him for many years. A strict Muslim and family man, he was the complete opposite of his brother, Prince Jefri. His Brunei lawyer, T.C. Chan, and I used to joke about how much more legal work we would have had if we had acted for the other brother, but in truth we were content at having such a reliable and appreciative client.

The work for Prince Mohamed was varied and interesting. I was given the task of supervising the architect who refurbished his house in Hampstead. This included reassuring the architect, while we both waited for the client to arrive to inspect the finished work for the first time. The architect was in a blue funk, and I had to tell him that, although capital punishment still existed in Brunei, he was safe in England. As it was, the Prince very much liked what had been done.

I was often called upon to satisfy rather unexpected requirements at short notice. One Saturday morning I received an early call from one of the secretaries. Eighteen of the Prince's entourage had just arrived at the house, and they needed to dry their clothes. How were they to do it? I pointed out that there was a fully equipped drying room, but the answer was that it was not big enough.

As soon as the shops opened, I bought about five metal clothes horses from a local household shop, and took them over in my car. I thought that would be the end of my duties, but I was wrong. I had to demonstrate how to set them up. I suppressed a cynical thought about this being the culmination of six years of dedicated legal education with a little difficulty. The early-morning call from the Prince's staff was quite a regular feature. The worst was a call at five one Sunday morning from Bangkok. I think that somebody had added rather than subtracted the time difference. The staff may have been importunate, but the Prince himself was always the soul of politeness and appreciation. I usually saw him dressed casually in a tracksuit, as he was a fitness fanatic. After one New Year's Eve was radically interrupted on his behalf, he presented me with a beautiful gold watch bearing the Brunei coat of arms. I wish more clients were as appreciative.

It was his brother, Prince Jefri, who was always in the news, not necessarily for the right reasons. He bought the jewellers, Aspreys, at a price which reflected the turnover and profit from his own purchases as their best customer, a strange kind of double-counting. Prince Mohamed, by contrast, apart from his duties as Foreign Minister for his country, shunned the limelight. It was therefore a great surprise when I was sent a copy of the French edition of *Paris Match*, which contained a lurid story about the antics and extravagances of Prince Mohamed of Brunei, until I realised that the magazine had completely confused the identities of the two brothers, and they were talking about Prince Jefri. Most of the article was a rehash of what had been written for many years about Prince Jefri, but one particular story about how he flew in Boeing 747s from Thailand filled with Thai prostitutes for himself and his guests at parties was new to me. None of this could remotely be applied to Prince Mohamed.

I asked the client what recompense he wanted as the article was so clearly defamatory. He told me that he did not want damages, and an apology would suffice. Letters requesting an apology remained unanswered. It is worthy of note that the international editions of *Paris Match* did not contain the offending article, so we were compelled to take action in France, where the publication occurred. I instructed the best recommended French defamation advocates, and they told me that proceedings had to be started within a month of publication of the offending issue. As the French lawyers told me nothing to the contrary, we worked on the date of publication shown in the actual issue, and the proceedings were filed in the Paris court just in time.

Paris Match disputed the action on the grounds that that the legitimate time for issuing proceedings had expired. They produced a scruffy, self-serving letter on their own headed notepaper which stated that actual publication was earlier. I was amazed when it became clear that the French court was going to accept this evidence without question. My French lawyers told me that I need not worry, as they were adding a second cause of action, *Atteinte à La Vie Privée*, which I translated as breach of the right of privacy, where the limitation period was twelve months, so we had no cause for alarm. They told me that this was common practice, accepted always by the court, to overcome the difficulty of the ridiculously short period allowed for starting the action in defamation cases.

The client did not want to attend the proceedings, but asked me to represent him at the hearing. The Paris courthouse is impressive, and the young female French advocates looked particularly provocative in their robes. There were three robed judges on the dais, and I had been told that the oral proceedings would last only thirty minutes, while the judges really made their decision based on the prior written submissions. I found the proceedings farcical. Our advocate droned on for fifteen minutes, then abruptly stopped. Their man did likewise. Nothing was said, so far as my limited French comprehended, which would influence the judges in any way. It was all a triumph of form over substance.

Judgement was reserved, and we had to wait a few weeks for the bombshell. Despite the clearest possible defamation, we had lost on technicalities. The defamation action had been submitted out of time and therefore failed. Furthermore, the court was not inclined to allow this issue to be circumvented by the use of the alternative action of *Atteinte à La Vie Privée*. Our action therefore failed totally, in spite of the prior reassuring words of our French advocates, who had nothing new to say on the subject.

I had the unenviable task of informing a valued and respected client that we had lost an open and shut case. I felt rather like the architect, whom I mentioned earlier. The Prince was, not surprisingly, extremely angry and upset, but fortunately not with me. He instructed me not to pay any more to the French lawyers. I urged him to appeal, but he had had enough of the travesty of French justice. I, for my part, felt ashamed that the French court should show such naked prejudice against a foreigner in protecting *Paris Match*, a French institution, against our action. It was not as if we were seeking damages. We only asked for an apology.

I do not believe that an English court would ever show prejudice in this manner against a foreigner seeking its protection, but I learned something that day about what goes on such a short distance away. If my client had been a French citizen, I am perfectly sure that the result would have been in our favour. I was fortunate that my relationship with the Prince was sufficiently strong to withstand this setback, and he remained a loyal client for many more years.

26

KENYA, YET AGAIN, AND SAN MARINO

Just When You Think You Know Your Client

I inherited Mrs Paccitti as a client when a partner left suddenly. The file did not tell me very much. It was a typical lazy lawyer's file, consisting of a claim against a law firm in Kenya, the validity of which was denied, following by a desultory correspondence getting nowhere. My former partner operated on what I call the 'alibi basis', by always writing the last letter and waiting for a reply. He was then in a position to placate the client, if asked for a progress report, though in truth there was never any progress.

I was particularly interested in the Kenya connection, so I asked the client to come in and see me, at the same time bringing her papers, as they were missing from the file. She was very much an English lady from the old colonial school. She had a tragic story to tell. Her husband had been killed when the Mau Mau blew up the Norfolk Hotel in Nairobi. She had received financial compensation from the Kenyan government of the time, which she had given to the managing clerk of her lawyers to invest for her. He had absconded with her money, and the law firm denied liability, as they had no records relating to her, let alone receipt of her money.

She dumped two carrier bags full of jumbled paperwork on my desk and gave me a tirade about the iniquities of the Kenyan law firm, and how she was making it her life's work to secure justice. After she left, I made some enquiries and established that the law firm in question was reputable and well founded. I then went about the business of putting the papers in order. Once I had extracted the extraneous material, which included a television licence, various bills and receipts, as well as circulars, I put it all into date order, and started reading. When clients complain about the size of their bills, I often counter by telling them of the many ways that they can make my life easier, including providing an orderly set of papers for me to read.

Everything was as inconclusive as I expected, until I suddenly came upon a scruffy hand-written receipt on the headed notepaper of the firm. I sent a photocopy to the client, who confirmed that the signature was that of the rogue managing clerk. I told her that I could continue the correspondence, introducing this hitherto undiscovered piece of evidence, or she could send me out to try to resolve the case in a face-to-face meeting. She agreed to the latter alternative, but the trip had to be on a very tight budget. I resolved to take Maggie, and we would bear a lot of the costs ourselves. This trip was very much a contrast to our previous lavishly funded visits.

In Nairobi, we had booked a room in a very cheap, so-called 'country club' on the outskirts of the city. Maggie was shattered by the journey and went to bed, but I felt like exploring the place. There were a number of black girls lolling about the reception area, and one of them offered to show me the sauna. It was like any other sauna, except it had a padded couch in it. She stood there expectantly, but I could not work out what she expected. A long time seemed to pass in silence, until I broke the spell, thanked her, and went off to my room. I thought about what she might have been expecting, but decided that I had a suspicious mind. Later that evening, when we went to have a drink in the bar, I discovered that my suspicions were almost certainly correct. The place was swarming with tarts, and obviously the reception girl expected to earn a little extra by freelancing with me in the sauna outside normal business hours.

I arranged an appointment to visit the senior partner of the law firm in Nairobi. Not surprisingly, he was difficult to persuade, as I was relying on an old and faded scrap of paper for my proof, signed by someone who was long gone from the firm in disgraceful circumstances. Eventually he agreed to refund the money plus interest, and a contribution to the client's costs. This was not the end of our problems, as Kenya was operating a regime of strict exchange control. Finally the Central Bank agreed to allow the money to be exported by equal instalments over four years.

Clients rarely understand the camaraderie that exists between lawyers. We can be at each other's throats one moment on behalf of our respective clients, and the best of friends the next. This was the situation here. Our former adversary took it upon himself to show us aspects of Kenyan life that we had previously not seen. A tour of Nairobi's industrial area was fascinating. Almost every major manufacturing company in the world had at least a distribution depot tucked away in this sprawling and remote area. It made me realise what a rich country Kenya is. A trip to the Nairobi races was an eye-opener of a different kind. The black race-goers, of whom there were many, were crammed into an insalubrious and ramshackle corrugated iron stand, where they made a constant and overwhelming racket. By contrast the whites enjoyed the perfectly situated and luxurious amenities of the Jockey Club. I felt as if an Osbert Lancaster cartoon had come to life. There was Major Featherstone-Trubshawe in his Panama hat, multi-coloured regimental blazer and bristling white moustache contrasting with his scarlet complexion sitting in the stand, on a seat which bore his name engraved on a well-polished brass plate. His lady wife was completely pale, and her skin had clearly never experienced the rays of the sun. She wore a hat which would have been fashionable at the time of Queen Mary. I was amazed that this way of life continued so long after the end of the Empire.

Our new friend, like most of the white community, lived in absolute splendour. His large white house was set in magnificent grounds with many trees and flowering shrubs that were unknown to me. At the bottom of the garden were a number of what I first thought to be large wooden rabbit hutches. I soon discovered that these were the houses of his black servants and their families. He told me that his obligation to look after them and their families financially lasted for life, rather like a private welfare state.

By contrast, we visited an extremely rich Ismaeli client, who was overjoyed that he had been chosen to act as the Aga Khan's chauffeur at the forthcoming celebrations to mark the anniversary of Kenyan independence. This struck me as no great honour, but he explained to me the awe and respect which the Aga Khan commanded among his people. I felt that the way they all contributed financially to their community, especially for schools and hospitals, was admirable. It is a little strange that the ruler himself cannot marry from among his people, so that in each generation the blood line becomes more diluted.

We chose the cheapest possible hotel for our few days' break at the coast. It was called the Shelley Beach, and we soon discovered why the locals referred to it as the 'Smelly Beach'. It proved to be a false economy, as I caught a painful ear infection from the pool. Nevertheless, it was a welcome break from the freezing English winter.

A few weeks before the trip, I had met a most interesting man at a drinks party. Ian Anderson was the head of the drug enforcement section of Customs at Heathrow. A big, raw-boned, redheaded Scotsman, he regaled me with stories about his work. One aspect which impressed me greatly was his statement that he had a photographic memory for faces and had filed away in his mind the images of all the villains in the drug world. We arrived back early in the morning at Heathrow to find the Customs area swarming with uniformed officers. Many arriving passengers were having their baggage ripped apart. I suddenly recognised Ian Anderson at the same time as he saw me. 'You there,' he shouted roughly, 'come over here.' I realised that he recognised my face, but his filing system was faulty and he had classified me with the villains. 'Hallo, Ian,' I replied tentatively. 'We met and talked at Alan Taylor's party a few weeks ago.' I saw recognition dawn, and we had an inconsequential chat. At the end of it, he held out his hand, and I had to overcome an almost pathological aversion to touching a uniformed Customs official before I could bring myself to shake it.

I was very much looking forward to seeing the client, as I thought she would be overjoyed at our success, especially as the costs of our trip were now covered by the fees contribution of the Kenyan law firm. I was wrong. She was angry and vituperative, and in fact walked out of our meeting. I had completely misjudged the client. She did not want a successful outcome. What she enjoyed was the continued battle. By my actions, I had destroyed the only reason for her continued existence. Perhaps my former partner, by merely going through the motions, understood more about human nature than I did. It was a considerable shock to my system.

It was not over yet. The client went to other lawyers, but it did not take me long to persuade them that I had done everything possible to satisfy a normal client. She then complained about my conduct to the Law Society, and once again I had no problem in dealing with the complaint. I had to admit to myself that the Law is a profession where you never stop learning about people.

*

The San Marino case also involved a voluminous file, which I inherited from a departed partner. It related to a dispute between our client, a company providing telecommunication services, and the San Marino Post and Telephone Service. The case had been rumbling on for years, and I was given file number six in the series. The lawyers had conducted a leisurely and inconclusive correspondence, while our client's equipment and money remained impounded.

I felt that a face-to-face meeting could bring matters to a conclusion, and the client agreed that I should make the effort. To save the client the cost of my travelling expenses, I scheduled my visit for a time when we were on holiday in Italy. My son, Paul, had just passed his driving test, so I thought this was a chance to give him some valuable driving experience. To get there, we took the autostrada via Bologna. It was the long way round, but it turned out to be far speedier. San Marino was like a film set for the capital of Ruritania. You see it in the distance, looming on a hilltop as if it were a fairy castle, and it appears and disappears as you zigzag up the steep road to the very top. Its brightly-clad soldiers and police reinforced the image, and I expected everybody to burst into song at any moment. The place was clearly set up for a tourist invasion. When the sun failed to shine in Rimini and the Adriatic coast below, you could expect the hordes to arrive to buy the acres of tourist tat on display everywhere.

I left Paul and my younger son, Edward, to see the sights and went off to my meeting. My opponents were delighted that my Italian was good enough to converse in it, and I knew that I had at least an hour to persuade them that my client's point of view was the correct one. In fact, it took only eighteen minutes before I was shaking hands and leaving, having achieved everything that the client required. It took me as long to find Paul and Edward. We had lunch, and decided to leave this tourist paradise as quickly as possible. As we now had plenty of time, we decided to drive back by taking the scenic route through Le Marche. Paul got plenty of driving practice on that journey, which took considerably more than five hours. The whole area seemed virtually deserted. There were pretty hilltop towns and villages, while the roads seemed to wind in all directions with no apparent rhyme or reason. Road signs were inadequate, and the map was not much better.

I expected that the client would be overjoyed at the result and that much new work would follow. I was wrong on both counts. The bill was paid by return, but I never heard from the client again. Will I ever understand human nature? I doubt it.

27

OLIVER CARRUTHERS

How One Man Can Open So Many Doors

When Anthony Sumption left the practice in 1964, I carried on in Mark Lane in the City in our expensive offices, but I soon realised that things had to change. With 'Big Daddy' gone, we were reliant on me to bring in the clients, as well as being the main processor of the work, but I just did not have Anthony's depth and range of connections. We had to economise, and the best economy was cheaper premises. John Carpenter House between Fleet Street and the Thames was ideal. It was much nearer the Law Courts, which meant that our litigation practice could be run more economically and efficiently. The building had been designed as apartments for the firemen who manned the adjoining fire station in Carmelite Street, but had been converted in a somewhat rudimentary manner into offices when the fire station closed down and the firemen were rehoused elsewhere. The developer, as well as the occupier of most of the building, was Hilary Halpern, a larger-than-life architect.

Until I met him, I had divided architects into two categories only: craftsmen and artists. I now had to add the category of showmen. Hilary loved to boast of his architectural accomplishments, which were many. One day, he said to me: 'I have built the tallest building in Britain. What is there left for me?' I replied very quietly: 'Jump off it.' He did not speak to me for the next six months.

The country was in one of its periodic recessions, which meant that architecture was in the doldrums, otherwise Hilary would have occupied the whole building. As it was, we took two floors on very good terms, and the one below us remained empty. The lift always attracted sarcastic comments from the more sophisticated clients, along the lines that it should be pensioned off and sold for scrap.

Eventually, the floor below was filled by Oliver Carruthers and his company, Gemini News Service, which was attempting to provide specifically for Africa the service which Reuters give the rest of the world. Oliver and I became good friends, and he transferred his legal work to me. He had a most interesting Anglo-American background. His father had been a Barclays Bank manager from East Anglia, who had been posted to New York, where he had met, fallen in love with and married an heiress from one of the original pilgrim families out of Boston, Massachusetts.

After Cambridge, Oliver joined the British Colonial Service, where he was posted to Tanganyika, and served up country as a district officer. On a rare visit from his superior, they were sitting on the veranda of his bungalow taking tea, when his boss's eye was drawn to a calendar on the wall headed 'J. Patel, Grocer and Sundrysman'. 'What's that on the wall, Carruthers?' 'It's a calendar, sir,' replied Oliver. 'No it's not! Take it down immediately! It's a bribe!' was the reply. It is not for nothing that the British Colonial Service gained its reputation for incorruptibility.

When Oliver eventually had had enough, and decided to resign, he had to visit his boss in the nearby town. 'We will miss you, Carruthers,' began the boss. 'Oh, sir,' replied Oliver, a lowly district officer, 'I did not know that I was so important.' 'No, Carruthers,' continued his boss. 'You don't understand. You are the last Carruthers left in the Colonial Service!'

Like so many who worked there, Oliver was left with an abiding love and passion for Africa, and that accounted for the existence of Gemini News Service. I learned more about Africa from the journalists whom Oliver employed, but my overseas trip with Oliver was to America, rather than Africa. Oliver and his siblings were beneficiaries under family trusts set up in Massachusetts many years before. These trusts were particularly inflexible, as remained the relevant trust law in Massachusetts. By contrast, the law in England had moved on, and it was possible to vary trusts here, to take into account the changes in modern life. The question was whether we could change Massachusetts' law, and I was going out with Oliver to try my luck.

The night before, I had mixed Bloody Marys for Maggie and myself in a particularly elegant, but extremely impractical, cocktail shaker from Aspreys, which was shaped like a champagne bottle, and hence almost impossible to clean efficiently inside. The next morning, Maggie woke up sick, but still accompanied me to the airport to see me off. I reserved my sickness until our arrival in America, and I was violently ill throughout our stay. Nevertheless, the job had to be done. I persuaded Oliver's local lawyers that the law could be changed, and gave them all the authorities and precedents they needed to do it. After all, I insisted, their law came from ours anyway, so there was no reason why they should not follow our changes. In the car afterwards, Oliver and I took a leaf out of Lizzie Bordon's book, singing, 'You *can* cut your settlement up in Massachusetts'.

Following the court hearing, where judgement was reserved, we all went for a formal lunch to Lochobers, an austerely wood-panelled fish restaurant. I was still suffering badly from a stomach ailment, so I asked the waiter for a recommendation for my condition. He suggested steamed lemon sole. When it arrived, I took one look at the plate, and made a dash for the washroom. When Oliver questioned me about this afterwards, I replied: 'It was either the sole or me.'

The mission was successfully accomplished and we made legal history in the Massachusetts courts by persuading the judge to make the changes in the family trusts which accorded with the beneficiaries' wishes, rather than leaving them trapped by the settlor's original restrictions, which bore little relevance to their needs today. We had a few very pleasant days in Cape Cod, staying in one of the family homes. I found local geography very confusing with Plymouth next door to Chatham, but the family were very hospitable and I felt I was on the set of one of those many Hollywood films which came out in the Depression to distract the people from the misery of their fate, where poor girl meets and marries rich boy, or vice versa.

On one of our Kenyan business trips, Maggie and I made a detour to go and look at Oliver's house at Malindi. He had invited us to stay, but there was no time. We drove down a long private road, stopped, and there it was in all its magnificence. Oliver was not there, so the servants gave us a tour. Afterwards, we returned to our car, but, while the engine started, we could not move, as I had managed to park in deep sand. We had to call the servants to push us out and onto the road.

Oliver continued to be a source of interesting introductions out of Africa. An Ashanti King used to make regular visits to London, and stay at a hotel in Chelsea. He would telephone me to come round. Once we had exchanged greetings, he would bring a soiled handkerchief out of his pocket and extract a number of gold, roughly finger-shaped nuggets from it. These I would take to Johnson Matthey, the assayers of precious metals near Hatton Garden, who would weigh them, and give me a cheque for their value. On one occasion, I suggested to Johnson Matthey that they should visit the King in his hotel, and weigh the nuggets there, but they assured me in all seriousness that they did not have portable scales that would do the job. It was clear that such an august and well-respected organisation expected the client to come to it, and never vice versa.

Everybody was happy with the arrangement, a perfectly legitimate one, which took place long before the dead hand of money laundering legislation. On one occasion, when I went to see the King, I had Paul and Edward with me. To entertain them, he put on his robes and crown and then allowed them to try them on. These visits continued for a number of years, but then abruptly ceased. I never heard from the King again, and I wonder to this day what happened to him. I fear the worst.

CONCLUSION

I have been re-reading what I have written so far, in the hope of finding some sort of coherent theme, or a common denominator, which would make some sense of my professional career, but sadly I have failed to find it. In my defence, I can reasonably say that all my trips were made in the interests of my clients and by and large helped to solve their problems. But having said that, everything that has happened has been based on seizing the opportunity of the moment, and there seems little or no causal connection. I was either in the right place at the right time, the wrong place at the right time, the right place at the wrong time, or, worst of all, the wrong place at the wrong time. At least a taxi driver knows where he is going when he picks up his fares. I did not even have that luxury.

*

On the subject of being in the wrong place at the wrong time, I was on a business trip to Israel when the first Gulf War began. I always loved the hectic gaiety of Tel Aviv, particularly on a Friday night. The fear caused by the knowledge that Saddam Hussain's Scud missiles had the city in its range was like a douche of ice-cold water. Everyone who could was packing up their cars with tents and sleeping bags, and heading off to the Negev Desert. British Airways, on which my return flight was booked, ceased flying to Israel, and I could not wait to get out of the place. It cost me $500 to bribe a travel agent to get me on a packed El Al flight to London. It was worth every cent.

*

Everybody of a certain age remembers where they were when the news came through of J.F. Kennedy's assassination. You can say the same for 9/11. Two days before, I was sitting in the transit lounge at Newark Airport admiring the Manhattan skyline in the sunset. The uncompromising severity of the twin towers of the World Trade Center particularly caught my eye. Two mornings later, I was in my room at the Amway Grand Hotel in Grand Rapids, Michigan, fixing appointments on the telephone to visit various clients in the area. I quite often phoned Mark Quigg in Grand Haven, so the sound of the local radio news announcer, when I was put on hold, in place of the more normal soothing music, was no surprise. What was surprising was the contents of the news bulletin. Instead of inconsequential information about little Johnny Smythe falling out of his kayak and banging his head on a rock, the announcer was droning on in a monotone about a plane hitting one of the towers of the World Trade Center, and how another plane was approaching and about to hit the other tower. I thought of the famous Orson Welles' broadcast, 'the Martians have landed', and of the panic that it created at the time. When Mark came on the line, I told him how bad it was that the announcer was spreading a false message that could cause a panic. 'Have you got a television in your room?' he asked. 'Yes,' I replied. 'Switch it on!' he commanded.

For most of the rest of the day, I sat on the edge of the bed, watching the terrible events of that morning over and over again. I took a break to get some fresh air, and walked along the river bank. I had the unworthy thought that UA93, as yet unaccounted for, was heading directly for me. The next day, I was due to give the keynote address at the annual meeting of the Michigan Bar Association in Lansing. I phoned the organiser to confirm that the meeting was cancelled, and was very surprised when he told me that they were going ahead with it. I had a lift next morning from a lawyer in the firm with which I was working, and I gave my speech, but with no enthusiasm, which was matched by the audience. Our thoughts were all elsewhere. My topic was the future of the legal profession. Frankly, I was more interested in the future of mankind.

I was due to fly on the next day to another conference in Washington DC, but that was obviously cancelled. I wanted to go home, but every form of transport was grounded. I could not even telephone my wife to reassure her. Eventually, I found a flight next day to Heathrow out of Detroit on North West Airlines, but the problem was getting from Lansing to Detroit, a distance of sixty miles. I offered to hire a car, but I was told, not in a jocular tone, that I would be shot on sight, as there was a ring of steel around Detroit Airport.

I was advised to go to Lansing Airport and wait for a plane. All passengers on local flights were told to go home, and a group of six of us were left, of whom one was a Red Cross worker trying to reach New York to help with the carnage, while the rest of us were trying to leave the country. Eventually a Boeing 727 arrived completely empty, and the six of us made the strange but short journey to Detroit. I was then taken to the international lounge for an interminable wait, but I did not care as I was going home. There were not many passengers in the lounge, but the situation soon changed as another flight to London was consolidated with ours. Because of the shutdown of transport generally, it was difficult, if not impossible, for aircrew to meet their flights. When we landed eventually at Heathrow, I did not follow the example of the Pope, and kiss the ground, but I was tempted.

*

I am sure that other lawyers writing a book of this nature would be able to point to a pattern, a pathway or a progression. I cannot do that. I am sure that I must have learned a lot along the way, but it is difficult to pinpoint precisely what it was. I have met and dealt with some extraordinary people of the greatest possible variety. I have had wonderful hospitality and friendship, when I had no right to expect it. I have been betrayed and stabbed in the back, when I could reasonably have anticipated better treatment. I doubt whether I am any better a judge of human nature now than I was at the outset of my professional career.

I suspect that, if I had it all to do again, I would make exactly the same mistakes, or at least very similar ones. I have made many friends in many strange places, and just a few enemies. I am not yet in the business of writing my own epitaph, and I hope I can put that subject to the back of my mind for many years yet. However, if I was writing it now, I think it would have to be:

'HE HAD FUN'